Praise for

A Recipe for Biblical Success

One thing you can always expect from Jason Coache is transparency. In this book he openly shares his frustrating experience as a person driven to be "successful." The other thing that I've come to expect from Jason is that he learns from his mistakes and grows from what he learns. This book is some of the wonderful fruit of that growth. If you are a driven person, his teaching can help you avoid hitting a hard dead end on your road to success. The biblical instruction in these pages will be life-changing for some.

—Dr. David A. Ridder, Senior Pastor, Bayside Chapel

***

A Recipe for Biblical Success is a much-needed book. Far too many Church Leaders are defining ministry in the wrong way. Jason, with careful insight and practical experience, gives us a plan for how to make ministry about serving God. This is a book I'll be giving to Pastors and Leaders I coach and mentor.

—Paul Johnson, Past Executive Vice President of Converge Worldwide and Pastor of Woodridge Church

***

It has been a joy to see Jason harness his God-given ambition through the joys and sorrows of life and ministry. He has lived the wisdom in this book. This is invaluable insight for weary travelers and wounded faith workers that will help reframe your vision and recapture your first love.

—Andy Needham, Regional VP, Converge Northeast

***

In a culture that highly values success, we can mistakenly adopt worldly perspectives and measures for success. When this happens, we may lose our true sense of purpose, misplace our values, and even lose ourselves and our families. Jason reminds us of the importance of returning to a biblical definition and measure of success, namely, "Biblical success is when God's heart and God's ways become my heart and my way." In this practical and helpful guide, Jason draws upon his own experience and demonstrates how the truth of the Word of God helps us to return to God's perspective on success and allows us to regain our true purpose. This inspiring and helpful book is much needed in our post-Covid ministry world.

—**Dr. Matt McAlack**, Director of Youth & Family Ministry Programs, Cairn University

***

As a "successful" business owner for over 35 years and now the President of an International Non-Profit serving Malawi, Africa - I wish I had this book when I first started. Defining success is something we always struggled with as a Christian-Operated Business. Jason does a masterful job in providing the proper perspective - biblical! His transparency and authenticity illuminate and softens the hard truths shared within this book. A must read for those who want to redefine and challenge themselves on what success looks like in both their personal and professional lives.

—**Steven Chartier**, President, Good Soil Partners

***

In this book Jason Coache shows the immense benefit of doing the hard work of self-reflection. His words are challenging. Through his own experiences, he shows that God sets a standard for our lives that is much different that we naturally assume. God's way is truly the better way, but it will require from us a changed mindset and dedicated effort in a heavenly direction. The chapters contain several powerful descriptions that will make you stop and think introspectively.

—**Brian Weber**, Regional President & Executive Minister, Converge Midatlantic

***

Authentic and helpful are the two words that come to mind after reading, *A Recipe for Biblical Success*. Jason's willingness to share his own journey is helpful and enlightening. Too often, we have traded what is really important to follow the dream of success the way the world defines it. Jason helps us identify the folly that comes from chasing the world and to rewrite the definition of true ministry, family, and leadership success.

—**Lee Stephenson**, Senior Pastor, Harvest Community Church

A RECIPE FOR
Biblical Success

*A Guide to Honor God in the Pursuit
of a Successful Life*

Jason Coache

Published by KHARIS PUBLISHING, imprint of KHARIS MEDIA LLC.

Copyright © 2023 Jason Coache

ISBN-13: 978-1-63746-190-7

ISBN-10: 1-63746-190-9

Library of Congress Control Number: 2022948624

Scriptures taken from THE HOLY BIBLE, ENGLISH STANDARD VERSION ® Copyright© 2001 by Crossway, a publishing ministry of Good News Publishers. Used by permission.

All KHARIS PUBLISHING products are available at special quantity discounts for bulk purchase for sales promotions, premiums, fund-raising, and educational needs. For details, contact:

Kharis Media LLC

Tel: 1-479-599-8657
support@kharispublishing.com
www.kharispublishing.com

To my Grandfather, in life and in death, you have taught me how
to keep Jesus as the main focus of my life. I am forever grateful
for the legacy you have passed on that seeks to honor the
King of Kings and Lord of Lords. You not only wrote
The Making of a Model, but you also lived it.

TABLE OF CONTENTS

INTRODUCTION

Is this where I give you my resume to convince you to read the book? Is this where I rattle off a funny story? I have stories. I have some fantastic metrics from my past. But why read this? Because I'm you. As I type, I've almost thrown my computer across the room three times because it keeps crapping out on me. I've got a wife, and while most of the time, life smells like roses, the occasional fart creeps in. We've got three kids who are amazing and different; the nerd, the jock, and the princess. They fight, love, make you laugh, and make you wonder what you were thinking about having kids–and all that during just one family dinner!

I'm you, navigating this crazy broken world, trying to lead a church while remaining a faithful Christian.

Wait, Jason, didn't you title this "introduction?" This sounds like an about the author! Yup. Yo, don't you know that the "about the author" typically comes at the end of the book? Yup. 'Forget that', I do things my way. Until an editor says we won't publish unless you put this in the back. Ok, then I'll conform. So here it is; yes, I'm starting the introduction with an "about the author." This is my first published book. I've written others that are undone and will never make it to the press. So you need to know me and why I'm writing this. The lens through which I view life has an impact on this book.

I'm an enneagram three. I have to make lists. I want to be productive. I want to be successful. I like working hard. I want my life to matter. The thought of failure could put me in a psych ward. It's in my making.

My church, Wellspring Church, launched with just under 600 people on March 7, 2017. Within a month, we had two full-timers and four part-timers. Within two years, we moved into a building and gave away $15K in gas and over 120,000 diapers to people in need. In my world, those are "above average" metrics. But it was also an incredible amount of pressure.

Then, in 2020, I plummeted mentally when I thought every area of my life hit failure levels. We are now under 200 people. We have two full-timers and three part-timers. I am 37 years old, and I feel like my best days are behind me. We have less of every possible metric that we could use to make us feel good, all while getting hit with the same magnified pressures everyone else is experiencing in the "new world." Does this make me less successful?

I recently attended the Dave Ramsey Leadership Summit. One of the statements made at the conference was this: "Your life will cross a finish line. Everything you are currently doing will bring you to that finish line. Are you going to cross the finish line you want to cross?" I don't know if it was because my executive pastor and best friend was on vacation or if I was in a mood, but my heart melted when I thought about my answer.

NO. If my life and church are to go unchanged, I will hate the finish line I cross at the end of my race. To change my life, I have to change the course of my actions. So, is this a mid-life crisis? Perhaps.

I'm in a career that LOVES comparison. How big is your church? How many salvations? How many are online? How many books have you written? How many followers do you have? How much are you getting paid? What is the giving like at your church? For me, this is the *pressure of measure.* This is where I put tons of pressure on myself to appear successful, measure up to the next guy, and, sadly, win. This is the dark side of my competitive nature. These questions drive the metrics. Do the metrics drive success? I can tell you they drive pressure. Some pressure is good. It keeps people driven. Too much pressure, however, can cause an explosion with a deadly impact. I have experienced the good side of pressure, but I have also experienced the dark side of pressure.

I look around at the celebrity pastors and feel unsuccessful. They've got more of everything. They have much larger numbers in answer to the questions I asked above. So, if *they* are the focal point—if their success is what I measure my own success to, I do not measure up. Yet, are they supposed to be my focus? Do "higher numbers" mean more success?

For a guy who's madly in love with Jesus and craves success, shouldn't Jesus be the lens through which I view success? How many of us are successful by the world's standards but not God's? How many of us would assume we will hear "well done good and faithful servant" because we are successful with metrics we've brought in from worldly thinking? Have we secularized our Christian metrics of success?

What we try to measure ourselves against becomes what we strive to be. For me, I compared myself to other pastors rather than Christ. Sadly, I have failed. I begged God to let me quit. I went on a four-hour walk, crying the entire time. Screaming at the same time. "God, I feel abandoned." "God, this is not what I signed up for." "God, I have nothing left." "God, I don't know how to move forward." "God, I don't want to do this anymore." That walk was a defining moment because I begged for a release, and God said no. He viewed my life differently while knowing where He was taking me. Today, I am thankful He said no. In many ways, I still feel like a failure. People quit when they reach that point. Yet, how often do we feel a way that God does not? If we define success differently than God does, we will feel like failure when God may not feel that same way.

So, what is this book? It's a recipe for biblical success. I have heard it said in church planting circles that "healthy things grow." Yet, growth isn't always a measure of success. It is simply *a measure*. I grew by 20 pounds during COVID. That wasn't success, that was sin. This is for driven Christians to gain an understanding of where to be driven, how to be driven, and how to honor Christ in a driven nature.

What is biblical success? I'm asking you. Pause and answer these questions: What would you say is a successful life?

What metrics would lead you to believe someone lived a successful life?

Having given that even 30 seconds of thought, I'm willing to bet some of our definitions and some of the metrics we came up with would render Christ unsuccessful. Metrics of a comfortable life? Jesus died naked, broke, and homeless. Lots of friends? Jesus died with few at the cross. Lead a significant entity, organization, or kingdom? Hard to lead when you are dead. This type of thinking and these types of metrics impacted the disciples, no? When Christ died, they saw failure. They wanted the big kingdom now. They wanted their Leader alive to lead. They thought they understood the words of Christ, but their reactions proved they had misunderstood them. Most left, and one killed himself. I know there is so much more to the disenfranchised disciples than just this, but one element was an improper view of success.

I've been there, disenfranchised, feeling like a failure according to the wrong metrics and wanting to *run*. I was disenfranchised, feeling like a failure by the incorrect metrics and wanting to *kill myself*. I don't say those words lightly. For people of my making, failure can drive us to the grave. Unfortunately, this is more of us in America than we'd like to think.

What is biblical success? It's not a big house when our Savior died homeless. It's not more books when our Savior didn't write a book. It's not winning a popularity contest when the crowd helped put our Savior to death. If we have the world's metrics for success, then at some level, we will have to do things in the world's ways to achieve their metrics. What do we do? Where do we look?

The Bible is always a great place to look as we define definitions! The biblical definition of success? *Biblical success is when God's heart and God's ways become my heart and my way.*

Here is what Proverbs 3:3-4 says:

> *Let not steadfast love and faithfulness forsake you; bind them around*
> *your neck; write them on the tablet of your heart. So you will find*
> *favor and good success in the sight of God and man.*

I want this. I want favor and good success with God and with man. Don't we all? Here is the rub, we do not want to accomplish it through the means stated above. We want the cookie without the baking. We want the butter without all the churning. But this is life, not a grocery store. I want to be successful in the eyes of God. I must do the work of God to achieve success as God defines success. To achieve the success God desires, I must live as God wants. Why?

Because Biblical success is when God's heart and
God's ways become my heart and my way.

The Recipe

"Let not steadfast love & faithfulness forsake you; bind them around your neck; write them on the tablet of your heart." (Proverbs 3:3)

Let's break down the recipe into four key ingredients. The first two are obvious. They are words that can be directly used to describe God. First, God is steadfast in love. God is faithful.

Just as these words describe God, they set the bar for how we are to live our lives. God is our bar, our standard. Don't strive to be better than the world around you, that is not a high bar. "At least I'm not in a gang." "I'm not an ax murderer." I've heard these two statements jokingly point to our desire to use the broken world around us to puff up our own success.

My best friend in high school was Josh. We played soccer, won a state championship, and hung out all the time: the typical, small-town best friendship. We were good kids that got into your average everyday troubles. [Hey Josh, remember that time you streaked from the fire station to the high school? Good times.] His famous line to his mom was, "Mom, I could be worse, I could be in a gang." The crazy thing? It worked most of the time! I grew up in Bow, New Hampshire. For all we knew, the nearest gang was like 700 miles away. I tried that on my mom, and she was unfazed for one major reason: we had a different lens through which we viewed life. We were a church-going family that simply had a different worldview.

"It could be worse" is not the standard Jesus set for us. You and I are broken people living in a broken world. Do you want to strive for Biblical success? Strive to be like Jesus! 1 John 2:6 says, "whoever says he abides in him ought to walk in the same way in which he walked." Jesus isn't asking us to be just a little above average, He wants us to live as He lived! This is what my mom knew. Jesus was the standard, not the bar set by the local gangs!

The ingredients that made up His life ought to make up our lives. His character must become our character. What defines my God must progressively define me! In short, we must live in a constant state of Godliness. Real simple. Book over. Live like God. Have a good day!

Except, it's not simple. It goes against everything that comes naturally to us! Humanity has had thousands of years with an infinite number of lives that have come and gone. All have had a chance to live perfectly. All but One failed—the Son of God. God is supernatural, which makes us "natural." Living like Jesus is not easy. Admit it's hard, then do the hard thing.

The first ingredients listed on the back of a bottle or food package are usually the main ingredients most prevalent in the food. The food would taste very different without it, certainly not as good. When I am super focused on my health, I read labels. There is undoubtedly a taste difference when sugar isn't a top three ingredient!

Our first ingredients? Steadfast love and faithfulness. These are the hard things, followed by two ingredients that help us do the hard thing: commitment and heart. Is there more to the Christian life? Of course. The verse is not meant to be a catch-all. The verse, like this book, is a guide. It's painting a picture of a (CUTE) successful Christian life from a 30,000-ft view. You'd describe your home with different details from 30,000 ft versus standing on the ground. In the coming chapters, we will discuss each of these ingredients in more detail providing Biblical examples and marks on how to live out the specific ingredient, but first a snapshot.

Steadfast love is perhaps the most significant attribute of our God. He is faithful, immovable, patient, enduring, and forgiving. It's how and why we can depend on God. You don't become steadfast in a moment. It is the culmination of moments that makes one steadfast. My God through the generations has been a steadfast God, and He will continue to do so for generations more. You get *one* generation: so be steadfast. *Where God has proven His steadfastness with a generational grind, we can only prove it with a daily grind.*

Faithfulness has correlations with steadfast love. The focus here is on trust. Faith is trust in the unseen. It is why faithful Noah built a boat before the rain. It is why faithful Abraham packed up everything and started moving before God showed him where He would land. *A faithful God is a trustworthy God.* God embodies a reliable nature. In trust for the King, the faithful depend on the King. As we find God faithful, God finds us faithful when we learn to trust and rely upon Him. *A faithful person is a trustworthy person.*

Commitment is the ingredient that is understood but often overlooked. It's not glamorous, but you know when it is missing. I once had to melt butter for some cookies I was making and left the butter in the microwave. Yup, those suckers tasted, um, sucky! I had overlooked a necessary ingredient, and I knew something was missing upon tasting the final product! Our verse describes commitment as "bind them around your neck." The neck is powerful, but it is often overlooked just as it is with commitment. It is fatal to take a bullet or arrow to the neck. Your neck doesn't "do" a lot, but you know when it hurts, and it can be crippling when something is wrong. Commitment is like this. It's easy to overlook commitment day in and day out. However, you will feel it the second commitment is out of place, you will feel it.

The last ingredient is the heart. This is the ingredient that brings the flavor! I make an award-winning mint chocolate chip cookie. The key is adding the mint flavoring last. It is the smallest ingredient but it packs the biggest punch. Heart, to a degree, is like this. The Pharisees in Jesus' day on the outside looked steadfast, loving, faithful, and committed. They had all the ingredients. So, what were they missing? Matthew 15:8 tells us their hearts were far from Him. Our verse mentions "the tablet of the heart." The tablet of the heart has the same permanency as a tattoo. It is an engraving. It is choosing pen over pencil, with no possibility of erasing. It is our *WHY.* Why be steadfast in love? Our hearts, as children of God, ought to long for God. Why be faithful in a faithless culture? Our hearts long for God. Why stay committed when everything in life pulls at our commitment? Our hearts long for God. Two people can act the same way, the one with a great heart–that is the child of God–and the one with no heart–and that is simply "the religious person." Our former (unsaved) heart of stone, now longs for God as His child!

Of particular note, Simon Sinek says to "start with why." Why doesn't the verse start with the heart? In short, I don't know. However, we have to remember that Proverbs are short little snippets. Solomon writes them as pearls of wisdom to make us think and guide a life well lived. So to start, we must not overthink. We are taking one verse, and with the scope of all of Scripture, we are examining and defining what it looks like to live a successful Christian life. So perhaps heart is mentioned last because it's what we should remember most. Maybe it's mentioned last for people like me who can say in pride, "steadfast love? Check. Faithful? Check. Committed? Check. Heart? Oh, I don't know."

Did you notice what is not mentioned in the ingredients list of our recipe for Biblical success? Money. Position. Title. Power. Location. If you are making cookies, you don't need yeast. If you are making chocolate chip brownies, you don't need frozen fruit. Those are not the key ingredients.

Are you giving God your very best? Are the ingredients the recipe is calling for the ingredients you are putting into the mixer? Have you left the butter in the microwave?

I love this list of ingredients because this is something we can all strive for in life. These are ingredients we can all make part of our everyday lives. They are a starting point and a focus for us all. The desired outcome demands a specific input. Want to live a successful Christian life? It doesn't require a dollar amount, a position in a church, a home in Israel, or even yielding power. There's no class to take or a number of good deeds to accomplish. There is not a specific amount of money you need to give. This means you can live a Biblically successful life...

... and never work in a church.
... and never be a missionary in Africa.
... on a small income where you trust God with your first fruits.

If we focus on executing this recipe with the four key ingredients, you will live a life of results.

The Results

So, you will find favor and good success in the sight of God and man. (Prov. 3:4)

Do X and achieve Y. If the cookie recipe calls for ten ingredients, a certain temperature to cook at, and a specific amount of time, and you do what is asked, you expect cookies. So here is what God says we can expect if we follow the recipe: favor, good success in the sight of God, and good success in the sight of man.

First, there is favor. This word is misused and misunderstood. Noah had favor. God's favor required him to build a boat. Mary had favor. God's favor led her to family struggles, a birth in a barn, hiding in Egypt, a sexually immoral reputation, and watching her oldest Son die on the cross. The truth is, we have all been raised to see favor differently. We see it as money, power, and a life of ease. Favor in God's world is more like a promotion that comes with additional work and greater expectations. The favored Christian is the one who was trusted with little and can now be trusted with more.

Then, there is success in God's eyes. This means to know the recipe and attack the recipe. Following the recipe leads to the desired result. God wants us to follow the recipe He has laid out for us and thankfully He has made the recipe known! The fool knows what ought to be done and does not do it. The wise and successful Christian desires to hear "well done, good and faithful servant." Follow the recipe He has given us, striving to hear these extraordinary words!

Lastly, there is success in the eyes of man. Men *will* persecute us. It is promised, so don't let it catch you by surprise. Yet even amid persecution, there are elements of Godly success that even the worldly man can't deny. Joseph's faithful living won over Pharaoh. Daniel's faithful living won over multiple rulers in Babylon. The faithfulness of the early church brought many to the name of Jesus, despite heavy persecution. The early Church knew extreme generosity, to lengths unheard of today. They sold their homes to give to the needy. Even if they didn't go so far as to sell their homes, they offered them up to people as a way to help. If you drive with traffic, you go relatively unnoticed. Yet, if you drive against traffic, no one will be able to ignore you. But don't expect everyone to love the way you are driving. You will be driving in the right direction as determined by God, blowing right past the "wrong way" signs our world has imposed. Live the loving, counter-cultural life God calls us to live, and you *will* be seen. Most will hate you, but some will want the God you serve.

If you want real results, you must do the real work. You can use your kid's fake plastic fruit to make fruit salad. It will look good but taste awful. Instead, use the real stuff to achieve what God wants you to achieve. The spiritual ingredients God is asking us to put in are for the results God wants to bring to our lives. The results are not power, fame, and money. They are better. They are real. They are lasting.

Favor with God and success in the sight of God and man! I want this.

This won't be accomplished overnight, but when the collection of all your nights comes to an end–when you cross the finish line your life is heading towards–how will God answer those questions?

This is a journey. HERE. WE. GO.

PART ONE

THE RECIPE

INGREDIENT #1: STEADFAST LOVE

"Let not steadfast love…"

"Success awaits those who steadfastly commit to
any requisite sacrifice." **Ken Poirot**

I want to make this sound sexy, you know? I mean if you just read the table of contents and jumped here, skipping the introduction, you are like "what? This sounds exciting!" P.S., go back and read the introduction. Love, faithfulness, commitment, and heart-come on, so lame! Steadfast love is a grind, it is work, it is relentless. Everyone told me to drop the word "sexy" from the opening paragraph, so I'm leaning in. The informal definition of sexy is "exciting; appealing." This is why steadfast love is perhaps the most essential ingredient. It forces us to ask, do I really want success as God defines success? We want what's sexy–God wants steadfast. A pursuit of each will land you in vastly different places.

I started with a very "sexy" story in the church planting world. When I hang with others who have started churches, telling "my story" makes grown men salivate. The Sunday before we launched, we used our marketing budget to give away free gas to our community. We had about a two-mile line. The cops got involved. I was on the news. Radio stations came. It was amazing—a dream. Next Sunday, at our launch, we had just under 600 people. We hoped for 400. That is the goal; start with 400 because only half will continue to week two, historically. With 400, you can settle in over 200 was the conventional wisdom of the day. We effectively birthed a teenager. The year before, I was a youth pastor with about 120 students. Now? A pastor of a church about 600 in size? Over 30 people committed their lives to Jesus that day. What?!!!!! The following Sunday, we had over 400 people, and we maintained that number for a couple of months. Success. Sexy. Numbers. Impact. By all accounts, I had earned the title of "a successful church planter."

Then the summer happened. The school we rented failed to tell us they didn't have "air conditioning." The building got hot–*real* hot. We had people leave and say, "I'll see you in September when it cools down." Two people passed out from the heat. Our numbers dropped to about 150. I felt like a failure. I wanted to crawl into a hole. I wanted to hide. I wanted to run. I was afraid. With the wild success of the start behind me, I felt like a failure in the present. But was I? Sure, there were plenty of lessons learned. But did God see me as a failure? No. In Christ, I may fail, but I am never a failure. But that does not mean that I don't feel like a failure from time to time. This was one of those times. In feeling like a failure, I felt like we lost the "sexy," and my response was to get "sexy" back.

That summer during staff meetings, our conversations were about new locations, driving attendance up, renting ice cream trucks, and buying portable AC units–all healthy discussions, to a degree. However, they did not include, "Hey team, God led us to this building, how do we remain steadfast through it?" I wasn't seeking what God was trying to teach me through it. I simply thought God wanted me to fight to get us back to what was.

Wrong views lead to wrong conclusions. It's what happened to Samuel. Saul turned out to be a dude who looked like a king but failed to have the Godly heart of a king. Samuel wanted to find a "sexy" king like the one that had just been a failure. He wanted image and prestige, and now he needed to add some integrity. So God leads him to a guy named Jesse. Most of Jesse's kids have the look, you know, they passed the "eye test." But again, wrong views lead to wrong conclusions. God led him to Jesse's youngest son, David. God saw the heart. God had a different "it" factor than Samuel had. God was looking for steadfast love, not some flashy outward appearance.

This was my problem. I had a flashy appearance and concluded that all the hard work was paying off. "My version of steadfast love led me to the flashy." Once it was all ripped away, my true heart was on full display. I'd been focusing on bringing the sexy back when I should have focused on steadfast love for my God and those around me. Steadfast love, for a guy like me, is hard. In my driven nature, I want results, and I want them now. God wants me to be steadfast, to love Him, and trust Him with the results. This has been a hard lesson and continues to be a hard lesson. So, we must see steadfast love as the way of God if we ever hope to make His ways our ways. We must if we want to be successful in His eyes. Why? Because *Biblical success is when God's heart and God's ways become my heart and my way.*

Steadfast Love: God's Heart and God's Way

The first Jewish audience reading this Proverb would have had their mind flooded with the steadfast love of God. They had experienced, tasted, and lived in it. Those large-scale beauties of life that, sure, you can read about, but it's only those who've experienced it really understand. My wife didn't see the ocean till she was in high school. My kids are a five-minute walk from the bay on the Jersey shore. When Ava was my kid's age, she could read about the ocean, but she could never really understand it in the way my kids are growing up to understand it. Many can read of a sunrise over the ocean and think that sounds nice. For my kids and me? I read of a sunrise and get lost thinking about my morning walks—the orange tint, the still waters, the clouds that seem to stand still, the birds cutting through the sky—and those ten minutes or so of utter peace. Reading of a sunrise causes me to pause and reflect on my own experiences. I'm not my wife as a child, simply wondering what it would be like, I've seen it firsthand.

It was not a foreign concept when the Jewish readers first read of *hesed* steadfast love. They had lived it. They had experienced it. This is God's loyal, faithful love for His people. This is covenant love.

Bob and Audrey Meisner define steadfast love as "Firm loyalty and unswerving dedication. Immovable, irrefutable, unchangeable, unalterable, and completely and utterly dependable and determined. Convinced that what I am doing is the right thing, and I refuse to ever give up."

The original audience would know this to be entirely true of God. So here is what would flood the mind of the original readers:

> **The Lord said to Moses, "Cut for yourself two tablets of stone like the first, and I will write on the tablets the words that were on the first tablets, which you broke. 2 Be ready by the morning, and come up in the morning to Mount Sinai, and present yourself there to me on the top of the mountain. 3 No one shall come up with you, and let no one be seen throughout all the mountain. Let no flocks or herds graze opposite that mountain." 4 So Moses cut two tablets of stone like the first. And he rose early in the morning and went up on Mount Sinai, as the Lord had commanded him, and took in his hand two tablets of stone. 5 The Lord descended in the cloud and stood with him there, and proclaimed the name of the Lord. 6 The Lord passed before him and proclaimed, "The Lord, the Lord, a God merciful and gracious, slow to anger, and abounding in steadfast love and faithfulness, 7 keeping steadfast love for thousands, forgiving iniquity and transgression and sin, but who will by no means clear the guilty, visiting the iniquity of the fathers on the children and the children's children, to the third and the fourth generation."** (Exodus 34:1-7)

God is giving the Law here for a second time. Remember what happened the first time? Moses came down off the mountain and saw the people he had just led out of Egypt worshiping a golden calf (Ex. 32). At the same time, God was showing them His faithfulness with the institution of the Law, they were unfaithful. The Lord, emphasized in double usage in verse 6, is merciful and gracious. This is exemplified as God gives His people a "second chance" even after the golden calf. The writing of this second tablet was a display that God had not and would not write them off. Did they deserve this second chance? No. That's grace. Undeserved second chances are both merciful and gracious.

How could you describe a God who gives second chances? Faithful and steadfast. Does this mean God will overlook sin? No, the Israelites were punished. As a result, members of their community died. The fact that God did not wipe them out completely meant He was merciful. Steadfast love and faithfulness may still be said in the context of punishment when the heartbeat is pushing forward. God displays love when He chooses to discipline as a way to refine us into His image! When we grow, we become an example to others.

God says His steadfast love would be known, seen, and felt through the generations. Catch this, it's important. Steadfast love is not weak love. It's faithful and long-suffering. Instead of writing them off, God kept them as His people knowing they would screw up throughout generations. Yes. His steadfast love through the generations with a people prone to wander is long-suffering and more faithful than our own. Now generations later, is not God still loving even during our "golden calf" moments?

In my life, there are sadly a few golden calf moments. Around 2013 (I may be off on the year), I had one of my lowest ministry moments. I was 29 and had been a youth pastor for five years or so. I had two kids, a happy marriage, and a successful ministry. Yet, I still hadn't "fully grown up." In my early 20s I drank as much as your typical college student. By 29, five years into my ministry, I was still drinking. Not as much, maybe, but far too often it ended in sinful drunkenness. Many of you reading this can have the occasional beer without getting drunk. Well done. For me, casual drinking led to intoxication too often.

One evening, I watched March Madness with a friend who was the husband of a co-worker in our church. Throughout the night, I'd had a few rum and cokes. When I stood up, it all rushed to my head. I was drunk. As I went to leave, I started running my mouth about issues within the church. I didn't say anything wrong, but I had said it in the wrong state, in the wrong context, and in the wrong manner. I hadn't been in control, and it led to major relational conflicts with people in leadership at the church. My sin created an instant mess.

The next day, I called my boss from my car in my driveway. I knew I had screwed up. I knew God had been telling me I needed to stop drinking, but

I ignored Him. I knew I wasn't in control, yet I didn't flee from my evil. I had hit rock bottom in this portion of my life. I wept. I broke down. I don't remember my boss' specific words, but I remember his tone. He had been gracious, caring, and kind. He had cared for the other parties impacted by the situation and me, and he showed it.

After the phone call ended, I walked in and told my wife. We cried. Her words, as you would expect if you knew my wife, were a little more firm than my boss' had been. Yet, she stuck by me and we pushed ahead. I told her I didn't know if I still had a job, that my boss had given me no indication of that, even through his kindness and graciousness. I had screwed up.

The next few months were filled with meetings to push me forward. More accurately, to encourage me forward. I met with the people I had wronged to own my wrong. I saw their tears, I felt their tears, and their tears moved me. There was a meeting with my pastor and one of the church elders. In it, I remember being thankful for my boss' protection. The elder had wanted to label me an alcoholic–to push me towards AA meetings and a recovery structure. My boss protected me, understanding that such a label wasn't fitting. This was a sin issue–but not a sin of addiction. We all have addictions. Some are of the clinical type, that of drugs demanding higher-level treatment. I was not dealing with an addiction to alcohol. If I had an extra $20 I was not spending it on liquor. I wasn't at the bar nightly. I was a social drinker who did not care about limits in the moment. I had a sin issue. I read "Saving Life of Christ" by Major W. Ian Thomas regularly meeting with my boss to discuss it. This book helped me focus on my identity in Christ. It reminded me that without Christ, I don't know how to love. Christ in me is where transformation begins. It focused on living my life as if Christ were living my life. I kept my job. I haven't touched alcohol since that sinful evening.

I was shown mercy and grace by all of the parties involved, especially by those in authority over me. The love I was shown was what encouraged me forward. I leaned into the steps I had to take, understood them and why I had to take them, and it; made me not want to repeat my foolishness. I am a better man for it, not only did I keep my job, but I grew in my position. The same boss who showed me the greatest mercy he could have in his position, who took the time to walk through this with me would, a year and a half later, show me grace when he asked me to start a church. As the sending church pastor, I was entrusted with 90 people and $275,000. Me, the guy who called him from my Chevy Aveo in the driveway of my house. That guy.

Allow me now, as a student and recipient of profound steadfast love, to share what I have found to be the distinguishing marks of those who would practice steadfast love.

7 Marks of Someone Successful in the Area of Steadfast Love

Principled

A person prone to emotional decisions will likely not be defined as a person of steadfast love. You've heard the saying, "rollercoaster of emotions." It is a saying for a reason. We, as a people, are all over the place. Our emotions, although real, are not always a real expression of our hearts. Have you ever said something that felt right at the moment, only to regret it moments later? No? Never with your spouse? Never with your kids? Never with a coworker?

So does being principled mean lacking emotion? No. Emotionless people often seem lethargic. The key is channeling our feelings in a principled way. Some of the most principled people I know are intensely emotional people. They have simply learned how to channel their feelings.

David's best decisions were not emotional, they were principled. Yet, David was highly emotional. David was a unique dude that could write poetry in the morning and then kill people mid-day. Different strokes for different folks I suppose!

David truly embodied this. In 1 Samuel 24, King Saul is seeking to kill David while David hides in caves with his men. Remember the story? King Saul had to go tinkle and as fate would have it, or better said, as God would have it, King Saul stumbled into the same cave where David was hiding. David, that guy that piled up all those Philistine foreskins and killed Goliath, had his enemy peeing right before him. David's men urge him to take the opportunity that God had put before him to kill his enemy. David sneaked up behind Saul and cut off a piece of his robe. This was not an opportunity from God to kill

Saul, it was an opportunity to prove himself principled. To be honorable and just. David fought through the emotions in the cave to do what was right. He let Saul go knowing it would lead to continued hardship. It did. What would you have felt as Saul hiked up his robe, utterly defenseless? For me, I would not have been thinking about honor, I would be thinking about vindication. What would your emotions have been telling you to do?

David had many situations like this throughout his life. Many times, emotions got the best of him, and he went against principles. Result? Sin. Here in the highs and lows of life, he experienced the steadfast love of the Lord. David, with the right heart, which we will get into later, allowed God to guide him through the highs and lows.

Psalm 13 is just one example of David resting in the steadfast love of the Lord;

> 1 How long, O Lord? Will you forget me forever? How long will you hide your face from me? 2 How long must I take counsel in my soul and have sorrow in my heart all the day? How long shall my enemy be exalted over me? 3 Consider and answer me, O Lord my God; light up my eyes, lest I sleep the sleep of death, 4 lest my enemy say, "I have prevailed over him," lest my foes rejoice because I am shaken. 5 But I have trusted in your steadfast love; my heart shall rejoice in your salvation. 6 I will sing to the Lord, because he has dealt bountifully with me.

David starts the Psalm off emotionally. Perhaps a time in his life when he was going from cave to cave. David sounds like he is on the run. He feels forgotten. He feels like his prayers are unheard. He feels "a way" about God. Then in verse 5, David goes back to the truth he knows of God. He may not feel God's steadfast nature in the chaos of this world, but he knows it. This knowledge, although he feels forgotten at times, helps him act principled in a cave and not kill the man trying to kill him as he is taking a leak.

Focused

Steadfast love can't just happen. You can stumble into love, but you can't stumble into steadfastness. Steadfast love is love proven over time, it can't be seen through one singular act. Think about it, could you fully convince another that you are a loving person based on one action? I am almost 15 years into my marriage. If I had to prove my love to my wife and could only point to the ring I bought her and the sacrifice of such an expensive gift, does that one-time gift really prove steadfast love? It is simply proof I did (past tense) something loving. You can prove to have done something loving while failing to prove to be loving.

Someone who is characterized by steadfast love must be *focused* on steadfast love. This is a character trait they are committed to and are actively pursuing regularly. Tim Stevens coined the saying, "What does love require of me?" When situations come up, a person focused on steadfast love should ask themselves some variations of that question. When your co-worker asks a favor of you, but it is "that coworker" who really annoys you; what does love require of you? When my son just accidentally ruined my expensive couch with a spill and now wants to play catch; what does love require of me? When someone with a sinful life that I do not agree with is being made fun of; what does love require of me? When a car cuts me off as I was in their blind spot; what does love require of me? The steadfast-loving, successful Christians will ask themselves this question many times a day. They are focused on choosing love.

We, as a people, do not choose to show steadfast love by default. By definition, loving like Jesus is supernatural, therefore, it does not come naturally to us. It is more natural for us to ignore people, to punch back, to drop the bag after just one mile because we don't want to go the full two, to lift ourselves up instead of you, etc. Yet opportunities to love are there for us if we look for them.

I'm writing this in my local coffee shop, there is a pesky fly bothering me. As I write this very section, a pastor friend and his family walk in. I used to work with him before starting my own church. Good friend. He recently battled some major health issues. It was so nice to see him enjoying his family on his pastoral sabbath. So, as I sit here writing this section on steadfast love, telling you the reader you can find opportunities to love if you look, I have an opportunity. So I pulled up my Venmo, sent him $10, and said, "get your precious girls some funnel cake" because they were heading to the boardwalk for the day. Had I not been writing this section, I very likely would not have sent money. My nature would have been to have a nice convo, then get back to my work. Nice convo, kind, but no act of love. My Venmo is kind of like a slush fund for me so it doesn't have an impact on my budget. The act of love took no effort, the effort was in the looking. It took an effort to find the opportunity to love and the courage to find a simple way to do it. Something small, right? but my hope is that if I did that daily, I might die known by steadfast love.

David had a similar moment at the beginning of 2 Samuel 9; "And David said, 'Is there still anyone left of the house of Saul, that I may show him kindness for Jonathan's sake?'" David was looking to show kindness. He was focused on it. He sought it out. He is the king of a powerful nation and this is his concern for the day? Yup. He is eventually told of a man named Mephibosheth who survived when Saul's family fled. He was injured in that experience as a young boy and remained lame in his later years. Yes, David had a dear friendship with Jonathan, Saul's son, but when a new king took the throne, it was typical for them to kill everyone from the previous regime. Why? Eliminate a potential future uprising. It's a dog-eat-dog world out there y'all. This is not only a relative of Jonathan, it is a relative of Saul, his enemy. Yet, what does love require of David? At this moment, he hears of someone in great need and chooses to give him land, people, and a seat at the table. In a moment, this man goes from being treated like a peasant to being treated like a prince. Why? David asked a question, he looked for an opportunity, and then he seized the opportunity.

What do you need to see a 'seizable opportunity?' Focus.

Defined

A person steadfast in love must know how to be loving. Our world loves the idea of love. Yet are we growing in love? Would we all define love the same way? If we define it differently, then we may do something loving that the person next to us would not consider to be loving. If we want to be successful in steadfast love, we must have the exact definition of love as God Himself.

About 4 years into my stint as a youth pastor, I took my youth leaders to a conference. During one of the sessions, the speaker made a point that has truly stuck with me ever since. The point she made in her talk was very simple yet truly profound. In the end, I had to think deeply and conclude that love did not define me as I thought it had. Her point was how do we know love? We know love by knowing Jesus (1 John 3:16). Said bluntly, God is love (1 John 4:16). So, Christ is defined by this attribute, love. He is love. Well, in that same book of the Bible we are told to walk as Christ walked (1 John 2:6). If we love, we will be known as His disciple (John 13:35)!

If love defines Him, it must define us. Easy enough until she went that final step. 1 Corinthians 13 has a powerful definition of love. It is read often at wedding ceremonies, but it was written in the context of church unity. Love is spoken about and exemplified throughout the Scriptures. Here, though, may be the most succinct definition. 1 Corinthians 13:4-7 states:

> 4 Love is patient and kind; love does not envy or boast; it is not arrogant 5 or rude. It does not insist on its own way; it is not irritable or resentful; 6 it does not rejoice at wrongdoing but rejoices with the truth. 7 Love bears all things, believes all things, hopes all things, endures all things.

So based on what we said earlier, this definition defines Jesus. It is Jesus. If that is true, and it is, then we could replace the word "love" with Jesus' name, and it would still be fitting. If we are commanded to walk as He walked, to walk in love (Ephesians 5:2), then we should also be able to insert our own names. This is what wrecked me at that conference as a youth pastor. We inserted our names to personalize it. This, as a definition of love, fails to define me. Better said, I fail to be defined by love. Here is how it would read for me:

Jason is patient and kind; Jason does not envy or boast; he is not arrogant or rude. He does not insist on his own way; he is not irritable or resentful; he does not rejoice at wrongdoing, but rejoices with the truth. Jason bears all things, believes all things, hopes all things, endures all things.

For me, the above is currently not true. It is aspirational. If I want to be defined by steadfast love, if I want to be successful in steadfast love, I've got work to do.

Sacrificial

My son once asked me what my favorite parable is. It's short so here it is Luke 17:7-10:

> 7 "Will any one of you who has a servant plowing or keeping sheep say to him when he has come in from the field, 'Come at once and recline at table? 8 Will he not rather say to him, 'Prepare supper for me, and dress properly, and serve me while I eat and drink, and afterward you will eat and drink'? 9 Does he thank the servant because he did what was commanded? 10 So you also, when you have done all that you were commanded, say, 'We are unworthy servants; we have only done what was our duty.'"

It's not one of the well-known parables. However, when I read this parable, I read it from the vantage point of a bond slave. A bond slave is a slave that comes to the end of their service and chooses to stay enslaved to their master. They willfully choose to continue because they believe in the greatness of their master. As Christ-followers we are bond slaves who see our Master as "worth it."

From that vantage point, I love my Master and I give Him my all. I don't choose when to serve. My service is not a matter of convenience. I serve my King throughout the day, and when I come home and there is an opportunity to serve further, I serve. When I have sacrificed what feels like so much, I don't say "Enough," I sacrifice more. Why? That is what a true slave does. That is what love requires of me. It is how I communicate love back to my Master. Here I say in my actions, You are worth more than anything else in my life!

Love is sacrifice. Love must willingly give it all. There is no greater love than one that would lay down his life for another according to Jesus in John 15:13. Love requires sacrifice. If you and I want to be successful in steadfast love, we must be consistently sacrificial.

My wife embodies sacrificial love for my family. She works long days as a real estate appraiser. Some days, her job is physically demanding as she goes house to house measuring and examining. Every day, the job is mentally draining for her. When she gets home, at most she may take five minutes to unwind. Then, it's dinner, get kids ready for sports, homework, etc. She gives her very best effort during the day as a successful real estate appraiser. Does her family get her leftovers? No. I see her sacrifice. We have never felt like we got leftovers. This is why I look at her and see love in what she does.

Consistent

A steadfast-loving person must be consistent. We have been dancing around this throughout the chapter. We have all but stated this. If you want to be defined as steadfast, you by nature, must be consistent. If you want to be defined as loving, you must be consistent. You cannot alternate between cruelty and love while expecting to be labeled as a loving person. To be steadfast is to be steady as you move ahead.

When are you the most inconsistent as a person? When are you the most unpredictable? Or when would people predict you will be "out of sorts?" In those moments, I'm willing to bet people would not see you as steadfast or loving (unless you're consistently cruel and abusive, then moving away from the norm is welcomed).

To be successful in steadfast love, you are not looking to be successful for a season. Steadfast love is exemplified over a lifetime. It is something that must become us. Losing weight is hard and keeping it off is even harder. I lost 120 at my peak of weight loss going from 275 to 155. Yesterday, I bumped into someone I had not seen for a few years. He had the guts to tap my stomach and say, "You are not what you once were but you've got some cushioning back." Yup, that really happened. It really rocked me. It is hard to keep weight off, his comment did not show an understanding of that hardship. Many people fail to keep weight off simply because they underestimate how hard it would be to keep it off. It is human nature to allow a few good days to give us a false sense of reality. Why? It is our pride. We think of ourselves more highly than we ought. Does one or two days of good eating outweigh five days of terrible eating? Pride says yes. Reality says of course not, but many of us live as it does.

If we are not consistent, we ruin what takes a lifetime to build. Warren Buffet is credited with having said, "It takes 20 years to build a reputation and five minutes to ruin it. If you think about that, you'll do things differently." Thankfully, God is more gracious than mankind.

When Solomon sinned and went after other gods, the kingdom was taken from him. Know who his comparable was? David. "Nevertheless, I will not take the whole kingdom out of his hand, but I will make him ruler all the days of his life, for the sake of David, my servant whom I chose, who kept my commandments and my statutes." (1 Kings 11:34) David. The one who murdered people, had an affair, and was severely punished by God multiple times throughout his life. Yet, David was consistent in feeling remorse, returning to God with repentance, and seeking growth. He got better. He was seen as steadfast.

A person of steadfast love is ultimately striving to get better. Success can make us complacent, and complacency will bring failure. Jericho was a huge win for Israel. Huge city with huge walls. They executed the battle plan God gave them with precision. Victory. Did they win the next battle? No. There was sin. Could it have been avoided? In Joshua 7, they only consult the Lord after they lose the battle. Joshua becomes steadfast in seeking God out before battles from that point on experiencing victory after victory. If we are constantly growing in steadfast love, we will be consistent in steadfast love.

Protective

If you want to be defined by steadfast love, you need to be there when it is needed most. Yes, you must be consistent in the daily grind–the everyday aspects of life. The question we are asking here is will you be there when it is needed most? Will you run, flee, or lean in? Will your son see you as steadfast if you miss the championship game, even though you made it to every practice? Will your friend see you as steadfast if you constantly leave them unread when they need to talk? When Proverbs 17:17 says, "A friend loves at all times, and a brother is born for adversity." After life has hit the fan, don't we often reflect on who proved to be true friends? Haven't we all gone into a troubling situation thinking so and so is a friend, only to realize in the midst of it that they are nowhere to be found? Graeme Wilson drove me an hour away to meet my parents traveling down to see my brother Justin the morning after his 14-month-old daughter passed away. I needed a friend because I had little ones at home, my parents were in a rush to get to my brother and it would not be wise for me to take a car when I did not know my return date. Graeme Wilson proved to be a friend in adversity and I will never forget it.

I bet you have friends you consider family. I bet when you describe the friendship to someone else you will say something like, "We've been through a lot together" or "he or she was there for me when I was…" How does this person make you feel? They probably make you feel protected and secure. Maybe just having them around makes you feel like everything is going to be ok. In Christ, we have these things as well; protection and security. Christ has established His rightful place in our lives and by resting our HOPE in Him we can feel secure and protected. Hebrews 6:19-20 says; "We have this as a sure and steadfast anchor of the soul, a hope that enters into the inner place behind the curtain,**20** where Jesus has gone as a forerunner on our behalf, having become a high priest forever after the order of Melchizedek."

Do you want to be known for steadfast love? Aim to be protective. Do your people trust you? Do they feel safe? Secure? If yes, these are the people who see you as a steadfast and loving person. When it comes to success, however, this is a quality that can be a double-edged sword. On a practical level, I cannot be this for everyone. I am human and cannot give my all to all. Truly, only God can. However, on the practical side, are there some? Do my close friends see me this way? Does my wife? My kids? Extended family? Does the organization I lead feel this way? If I die having these people see me as protective, trustworthy, secure, and so on, then I will die successful in the eyes of people who experience such things firsthand. Is there anyone who can articulate my steadfast loving nature? If yes, their testimony of me will help others know this even though they never experienced it themselves.

Immovable

Immovable is perhaps the last word that comes to mind when I think of a steadfast person. However, in 1 Corinthians 15:58, these words are linked together. It reads, "Therefore, my beloved brothers, be steadfast, immovable, always abounding in the work of the Lord, knowing that in the Lord your labor is not in vain." For those that strive to live successful lives, this should be on your "verses to memorize" list. Want your life to count? Don't want to get caught in a cycle of vain efforts? Be steadfast and immovable.

A steadfast person is moving forward at a steady pace. Each step of the journey is getting harder and harder. Finally, you are slowing down, and the person behind you yells, "be steadfast, keep going." You muscle the next step and the next one where you finally hit that finish line. How can immovable be related to steadfastness?

You can't move me. I'm in my spot. I will not be moved. I am steadfast. Cool, way to be you, macho man! Thanks. Your son is pushing you away, but you keep coming back showing him the love he may not deserve, you are being steadfast in love. When someone asks you to stay put, and you do so in a literal sense, you love them in your response. When you look at someone and say, "I'm not going anywhere," you are being immovable and steadfast. When my wife looked at me and said things like "in sickness and health, till death do us part, faithful to you as long as we both shall live," she was communicating to me that she would be immovable and steadfast in our relationship. She meant it then. I meant it then. We both still do. This is what love requires of us.

When God has called you to be a part of a church and the enemy is attacking you, you want to quit, you want to run, you want to go where the grass is greener. No, you are steadfast. You are not moving. You will not move, you will not run. You will stay put because God has called you to this SPOT. Be steadfast. Love requires you to stay: stay you will. HERE, here is where God has called me and I will be steadfast. Hold the hill, your labor is not in vain. Be steadfast and immovable.

Read the verse for this section again from 1 Corinthians 15:58, "Therefore, my beloved brothers, be steadfast, immovable, always abounding in the work of the Lord, knowing that in the Lord your labor is not in vain." This is a life verse for me. This concept of steadfast love for God, in being immovable, is something I keep coming back to. When I wanted to quit my current position, when a 'friend' wrote a letter expressing why she felt I should lose my job to our elder team, I wanted to be *moveable*. In the midst of such a hard year, I simply did not have any fight left in me. A phone call with my Dad served to keep me in the game. He said, "Jason, where are you? Where is the Jason that does not take crap from anyone? Where is the Jason God used to build this church? Where is the Jason that will look at whomever and say, THIS IS MY CHURCH I'LL BE DARN IF I LET ANYONE TAKE IT FROM ME? Jason, fight for this." I hung up the phone and went on a prayer walk. This very thought came to mind. I asked God when I started my church, "God, I will start this church, but I do not want to be a church planter. I want to die with this church, not bounce all over the place." So far, God has said yes despite me emotionally going back on that prayer request. Through Wellspring and the call on my life, I am learning to develop steadfast love and immovability. Why? I want to be more like Jesus.

The Example of Jesus

Therefore, since we are surrounded by so great a cloud of witnesses, let us also lay aside every weight, and sin which clings so closely, and let us run with endurance the race that is set before us, 2 looking to Jesus, the founder and perfecter of our faith, who for the joy that was set before him endured the cross, despising the shame, and is seated at the right hand of the throne of God. Hebrews 12:1-2

I love the TV show "Alone." It is about 10 people that get dropped off into the wilderness in different spots with limited gear, each of them competing to be the person who can survive on their own the longest. Each season I am struck by the people who simply can not endure being alone. Before they are left, each one is given a satellite phone they can use to "tap out" when they want to be done. Once they call and tap out, a crew is immediately sent out to extract the contestant and they are eliminated from the competition. Early in the season, contestants typically use the phone because they are scared, injured, or have realized they are in over their heads. Later, the contestants start using it because they feel they cannot endure being alone any longer. They lose their desire to go on. They miss home. They miss their family and being with them becomes more important than money. They decide it is no longer worth it to endure and they tap out. Why wouldn't they? The 'going has gotten tough' and all they have to do to tap out is swipe a few keys with the tips of their fingers and this can all be over. They can be eating cheeseburgers by the end of the day. Steadfastness has a way of testing our endurance.

A word we have not used up until this point is enduring. It's a related word to many of the character marks we listed above. If you aim to be immovable, there is the potential you will need to endure hardships that will try to move you. If you are trying to be protective, endurance of strength may be required of you. If you are steady and consistent through the journey of life and in your faith, you will be able to endure the challenges of life. The enduring nature of Jesus is proof of His steadfast love for you and me. He did not tap out.

The greatest example of love humanity has is in the person of Jesus. God's love put Jesus on a mission. Love for the Father motivated the obedience of Christ. In leaving the glory of Heaven to walk among the filth of mankind, Jesus endured here for over 33 years. In the garden, the night of His arrest, He prayed to His Father asking for another way (Matthew 26:39). Yet, His willingness to endure was seen in His willingness to elevate the Father's will over His will. And so He pressed on. He reminded Peter and the others that if He wanted out, He could get a legion of angels to come (Matthew 26:53), but He didn't. He pressed on. When they insulted Him, He pressed on. When they punched Him, He pressed on. When they whipped Him, He pressed on. When He couldn't physically carry the cross anymore, He pressed on, step by step, up the hill, even as another carried those wooden beams. While on the cross, nails pierced His hands and feet. Every breath was a true labor of love, putting pressure on those nails, raking his already ripped open back over the rugged wooden cross. Yet, my Jesus pressed on. He stayed on. He never tapped out.

Why? We must ask why. Why did Jesus endure? Because He loves you and me. It was a joy to obey the Father. To know of all those who would one day place their faith in Him. Joy, unspeakable joy, of what was to come kept my Jesus on that cross and motivated Him to endure. The steadfast love of the Lord endures forever (Psalm 136:1)! The steadfast love of my Jesus is an enduring love. It is finished because Jesus endured to the end. The steadfast love of Jesus meant mission accomplished and job complete. The steadfast love of Jesus meant Satan had been defeated, Jesus won the day, and He was, in a word; successful.

What is Biblical success? *Biblical success is when God's heart and God's ways become my heart and my way.* Want to be successful in the eyes of God? Be a person characterized by steadfast love.

INGREDIENT #1: STEADFAST LOVE
BIBLICAL CASE STUDY

"Let not steadfast love…"

"Turn your tears into joy, stay focused, be steadfast in the storms, (for) they don't last forever" **Stan the Man**

Growing up, my brothers and I each got a gift from Great Grandma for every Christmas and birthday. I have no memory of meeting her, as she lived on the opposite coast. She lived to be nearly 100 and never missed those gift opportunities. Impressive–but was it steadfast? Her gifts were unique. So unique that it became required in our house to respond after opening her gifts with, "Thank you, I love it, it's terrific." She would sometimes give us books with dollar bills scattered throughout. We never read the books, but the cash was cool. My brother was 13 when he got a Popeye and Olive Oil video, which he had opened surrounded by friends on his birthday. He was mortified, but still said, "Thank you, I love it, it's terrific." I was 14 when I opened up a smoking' locomotive from her for Christmas. Literally. A toy train that smoked, went in circles, and went choo-choo! 14–I was 14!

Steadfast for sure but, despite the best of intentions, it showed a disconnect of knowledge. She didn't know us. No bigs. We understood. Now, if my wife got me gifts like that? Constant frustration because it would show she does not know me in a way fitting to the relationship. Thankfully she doesn't. Recently, she got me Goo Goo Dolls tickets, a band from the 90's. It shows she knows I'm a 90's kid and knows the music I like. Her gift displays knowledge.

How many of us, maybe with great intentions like my Great Grandma, think we are giving God what He wants? What about what we know of God, makes us think that what we are offering is what He wants? Is there any chance that we are being steadfast while giving gifts that show we do not understand the relationship? Sometimes we think we can go through the motions expecting to put God in motion. We do all this religious work day in and day out, thinking our religious effort will get us a gold star. But then when life happens, we feel like God ain't moving, and nor does He care. In those moments we become complacent. Here is the deal though, what ends with complacency starts with a lack of competency.

We can't know what God wants if we don't know God. To respond as God wants us to respond, we must know Him. This is perhaps most magnified when we have done something wrong. We own it and try to respond in the manner we think He would want us to. We say more prayers, give more money, read more, love His people, etc. We go through the motions hoping to satisfy God. We think we can wait it out when God wants us to *wade it out.* When we respond to God with heartless sacrifice or a "wait it out" attitude, it shows we do not know God and therefore do not understand love.

If there was ever a people group to struggle with this, it was Israel. God's chosen people were notorious for being God's chosen headache. They were royal screw-ups who thankfully served a God who is royally gracious! Like the time Moses is up on the mountain and God is giving him the law to share with the people, boundaries on how best to worship Him, they grow impatient waiting for Moses to return, so naturally, they take all the gold God gave them from Egypt and put it in a fire. They craft a golden image out of it and celebrate their new, self-made god, giving *it* credit for taking them out of Egypt. How insulting! Right there, see? I would have started fresh and found new chosen people. Thankfully, I'm not God. He's better at it. He's gracious.

Let's look at another example. In the book of Hosea, God's people are back and forth between worshiping God and Baal, the storm god. They have moments where they rely on God and moments where they try to create military alliances, just in case God doesn't show up. God is brewing with anger. Even though they are in the midst of judgment already for screwing up before, greater judgment is coming. We find this at the start of Hosea 6.

> "Come, let us return to the Lord;
>   for he has torn us, that he may heal us;
> he has struck us down, and he will bind us up.
>   After two days he will revive us;
>   on the third day, he will raise us up,
>   that we may live before him.
>   Let us know; let us press on to know the Lord;
>   his going out is sure as the dawn;
>   he will come to us as the showers,
>   as the spring rains that water the earth."
> Hosea 6:1-3

Commentaries argue about who is speaking in these verses, Hosea or the priests? For our purpose, we can say that it is the leadership of Israel speaking on behalf of the people. They hope the people will accept this as their confession, owning the decision to stop and seek God. They are hoping to persuade the people to repent before they die from God's judgment.

Israel has rebelled. They have looked to the false god Baal for help. God, through Hosea, has been saying judgment is coming. Now that they are in the midst of it, they take a moment (verses 1-3) to confess their sins. Amid God's judgment, they desire to return. They acknowledge that God is sovereign and trust His ability to deliver them. There is confidence and expectation in God's response. Their motivation was not love for God, it was love for self. If we do the right thing, God will relent. Here is the problem with that thinking; it's contract thinking: not relational thinking.

We will do X to open up Y. We need to reject Baalism. We need to stop creating alliances with foreign powers. We need to trust God alone. This sounds good. This sounds positive. Will God see it this way? Will God feel this way if the motivation is simply to end judgment? Would they be willing to do what is right simply *because* it is right?

They are right to put themselves in the hands of God since they've failed to do that up to this point. Their desire for revival is good. God brings revival. Even the 2-3 days they mention has correlations with ceremonial rituals behind death. They are looking to go low so God can raise them up. They understand that it is better to be in the hands of God's potential mercy than to keep sinning and know His wrath. They find God to be reliable, so His mercy can be trusted. Again, all this sounds good and truthful—but what were they missing?

Indeed truthful, but can we demand it? Can we assume it? They seek healing while confessing sin. However, they make no mention of their specific sin. Can one repent without naming their sin? That is about as meaningful as saying, "I'm sorry for the way you took it." Or "I'm sorry you took what I said the wrong way." These apologies take no ownership. Ironically, it puts ownership on the offended party. It is insulting. The Israelites want revival but speak as if God is the one needing to be revived. My friends, my Jesus is alive and well. If anyone, ever, is in need of being revived, it is ALWAYS you and I! The desire for revival without the desire for life change is *insulting to our God*.

There is an infamous scene from the movie *The Breakup* starring Vince Vaughn and Jennifer Aniston. He works a day job dealing with people, leading duck boat tours around Chicago. She works full-time, if I remember correctly, in the fashion industry. Each working a full day, they come home to get ready for a dinner party. A little tension starts to brew as he doesn't want to help and really wants to kick back after a long day. The dinner party comes and goes. It was a great time. He, the people person, crushes it. When dinner ends and the guests leave, obviously the clean-up begins. This is where he derails. He plays video games. He does not help and she communicates her displeasure. As the explosion nears, he decides he will help… with attitude. Here's how their conversation goes:

"Fine, I'll help you with the dishes," he says.

"No, that is not what I want," she responds.

"That is what you said you wanted."

"No, I want you to *want* to do the dishes."

"Why would I *want* to do the dishes?"

"See, that's the problem."

That is our problem. If you were to ask the girlfriend, as the boyfriend gets up off the couch, if she felt loved at that moment, she would probably say, "NO!" But if you were to ask the boyfriend in that same moment if he loves her, with attitude he'd probably say, "Ya, I'm doing the dishes, aren't I?!" He thinks he's acting loving, yet with the attitude and motivation (to get her off his back), she does not *feel* loved. It is not how she wants to be loved.

If you were to ask Israel at this moment if they love God they would say "yes, were doing XYZ and now they are willing to do ABC." But is this how God wants to be loved? Does God feel loved in their scripted response? Would you feel loved if the offender dictated to you how you would be moving forward? Would you feel loved if the person taking ownership of the wrong also dictated how you *both* should act moving forward? What gives them the right, in light of the wrongs they have committed, to do such a thing?

Israel believes a change of action will bring about a change of heart from God. God responds by correcting their thinking. "No. You must not 'have to' have a change of heart leading to a change of action and you may experience mercy." What do they have to offer God that He needs? What leverage do they have? How does an attitude of "I'll just wait it out" honor God? You pay fines and move on with the government. But in a relationship, there is sorrow, there is a life change, there is a change of perspective, there is ownership, there is an "I'm sorry," there is a change of heart. There is a whole lot more than "wait it out" or pay the fine. Israel communicated they wanted to be steadfast but lacked the second word, love. They wanted to be in prison, doing well in prison, being steadfast towards the end of their sentence. However, with no heart change, waiting it out simply leads to repeating behaviors. Here is God's response:

> What shall I do with you, O Ephraim?
> What shall I do with you, O Judah?
> Your love is like a morning cloud,
> like the dew that goes early away.
> Therefore I have hewn them by the prophets;
> I have slain them by the words of my mouth,
> and my judgment goes forth as the light.
> For I desire steadfast love and not sacrifice,
> the knowledge of God rather than burnt offerings.
> Hosea 6:4-6

God tells Israel their words and sacrifices are like the dew in the morning, and their love lasts as long as the morning clouds—neither of which last long. God is painting a picture of their character as He sees it. God reminds them of their actions historically. We do this, don't we? We think ourselves more steadfast than we are. We can have a few good days on a new diet and suddenly feel like we are health experts. Mankind, of which you and I are a part of, always has an inflated view of ourselves. We see ourselves as loyal and good for it, but we aren't. We are like the kid walking into the lunch room looking to borrow money saying "I'm good for it," when yesterday, the day before yesterday, and even the day before that, he wasn't. Now, all of a sudden, he's good for it? It would be foolish to believe him.

God sees that Israel's motivation is self-serving. They want to live this way now only to get out of trouble. *I want you to want to do the dishes.* God wants to be wanted. God wants them to enjoy Him and not simply to get out of trouble. Mercy is the pathway to grace. Mercy is not receiving what is deserved. Grace is receiving what is undeserved. Mercy is where we seek forgiveness, own our wrong, hoping against all hope that mercy may be extended. There is no mercy without repentance. Based on mercy, grace can be extended. God in His goodness often extends His favor out of His mercy. God wants a changed heart, a heart that worships Him. A heart that is not fleeting or selfish. Going through the religious motions just hoping to put Him in motion in your life, will never cut it with God. He wants you to want to do the dishes!

So you want revival? Revival is not looking to our living Savior hoping our actions will revive Him. Revival starts with us, the dead, the broken, and the sinful. In Christ, we have resurrection power. Have you died to self? Are you sleeping? Revival is when the sleeping are spiritually awakened. Perhaps pause now and in the quietness of where you are at, pray something along these lines: *God take my heart, take all of me, and change me from the inside out. God, I give you a blank piece of paper. You dictate the terms. Lord, have Your way in me.*

As the story goes there was a U.S. Lutheran bishop taking a season to visit different parishes around the county. When stopping into one Californian parish, he noticed a vibrant red and orange banner on the wall. Through the images of fire burning, it said, "Come Holy Spirit. Hallelujah." Now, that in and of itself is not that noteworthy. Plenty of churches have decorative banners. What caught the bishop's attention was the fire extinguisher underneath the banner. It was this image that prompted the bishop to talk to the people about spiritual renewal.

This story shares imagery I feel is all too real in the church and in our personal lives. We want revival, we want renewal, we want some of that Holy Spirit fire all while walking around with a fire extinguisher. We welcome God in and let Him have His way, but the moment it becomes sacrificial and uncomfortable, we run for the fire extinguisher. We will go to church until the pastor challenges something in our lives, then we reach for the fire extinguisher. We will pray for patience until our spouse pushes it–fire extinguisher. We ask God for financial blessing, but when it comes to giving back to Him? Fire extinguisher. Ultimately, we want revival without life change. WHAT IS THAT? To want revival without the desire to change is to not want revival in the first place.

We start this way. We say yes to Jesus, are on fire for Him, and doing all the right things. Over time things relax a little. We keep doing the right things and for the most part, are still motivated by love for God, but we show no growth. We think we are done growing and that we understand enough of God. Can we ever fully know God here on earth? Will we ever be completely like Christ here on earth? No. So there is room for growth. There will always be room to know God deeper. There will always be room to live more like Him. Our pursuit of steadfast love towards God must go deeper daily.

How are you growing in steadfast love towards God? Are you growing in consistency? Are you always looking for opportunities to be generous? Do you wake up and ask God, "where do I lack steadfast love?" Are you increasingly forgiving? When God reveals areas of your life that do not look like the life of Christ, are you still addressing those areas? When faced with those gray areas in life, are you asking, "what does love require of me?" Are you sacrificing to get something from God or to be more like His Son? The best response to our God is to love like our God.

What is revival? Revival is when people choose God. Revival is when people choose to return to Him. Revival is experiencing God who is real, living, and powerful. Revival is NOT reform. Revival is not the transition from rebel to legalist. Revival is the transformation of the heart, where one lives in steadfast love for the King! Revival is when the spiritually dead become spiritually alive. Revival is about living for the name of God over the name of self. Revival is when we hand God our brokenness allowing Him to put us back together again. Revival is living to bring glory to God in every decision you make. Revival encourages those who are dead, cold, and walking away from God, to return to a state of joy, peace, and obedience to Christ.

Want revival? Choose Christ. Now. The next decision. Then the next decision. Keep choosing Christ. Remember, when we die, we all cross the finish line. Revival brings redirection, guiding us towards a better finish line. Choose Christ. He's there waiting when you cross that final finish line.

When you die and meet Christ, there is this question that gets asked in Christian circles: "what's the first question you are going to ask Christ?" I've heard countless people tell me that the first thing they want to ask is, "free will? Really! Why did You have to give us free will?" Here is how I envision Christ responding, "So you would choose me." If Christ didn't give us the ability to choose, then we are robotic. If He forces us to love Him, is that love? Because, in our culture, when a more powerful being forces his love upon another, that is jail time, and rightfully so. But the love that is extended, accepted, chosen, and reciprocated, there is something beautiful about it. So, revival? It is using our free will to choose Christ over and over again. Do this, and you have found not only the essence of revival but also steadfast love.

Tonight, I have to take one of my kids to MJ's for dinner. MJ's is a restaurant by my house, on the bay, and a manageable walk. It's about a mile and a half-round trip. So, it makes for a nice dinner and a walk. Also, it makes for a great "life talk" type family moment.

My wife Ava and I had a powerful moment like this about four years ago. Three kids, two stressful jobs, a booming church plant, and all the stress and pressure a couple could manage. We were fighting. To this day, neither one of us could describe what we were fighting about but we can both remember this dinner because it is the dinner that saved our marriage. We were both kind of just done. We didn't hate each other, but we were not connecting and it became two people just existing.

So, we went for a walk. We got a sitter and said in principle, "I love you enough to find a fix." We were at rock bottom emotionally so with nothing to lose, we laid it all out. The end result? We were not loving the other the way they wanted to receive love. Familiar with Gary Chapman? He suggests there are five love languages and people tend to desire one or two of them naturally. They are words of affirmation, quality time, physical touch, acts of service, and receiving gifts. My wife's number one love language is physical touch. Want to know my least desirable love language? Physical touch. Through conversation, we acknowledged we were not loving each other the way the other person wanted to receive love. What we were doing, and in some cases not doing, was actually depleting the love tank. We walked away (literally) from that dinner committed to sacrificially loving each other in ways that may or may not come naturally to us. It has saved our marriage. Now, I prioritize the impromptu hug. Will I ever hug Ava as much as she desires? No. Does she see me trying? I hope so. I see her words on social media and in text messages, realizing this does not come naturally to her, so they are all the more meaningful to me.

God delights in love done right.

What does God desire? He is gracious so He makes it known- steadfast love and knowledge. This highlights two critical elements as we close out this chapter: motivation and growth. Anyone can be steadfast, but few display steadfast love. Humanity is strong in its own right. Many have grit. Many are motivated by love. Love for self can lead us to accomplish the impossible through steadfast efforts. Few look to God in loving worship desiring Him to do the impossible through us.

Steadfast love is not motivated by simply waiting out a punishment. Steadfast love doesn't go with an "I have to" but rather an "I get to." There is a word for people who come to God willing to sacrifice to get something in return. Religious. That is the definition of religion. You act a way so God will bring good your way. When we are steadfast in our faith, motivated by love for our God, we are practicing worship. Steadfast love wants to do the dishes. Steadfast love wants to love another the way they will receive love. Steadfast love does not tell another, especially God, this is how you will receive love. Steadfast love asks, "how do I best love you?" It gives the other person a clean slate and then does that thing.

How do you respond to God when you are at odds with Him? Perhaps like Ava and I, it's time to have a meal with God saying, "what does love look like in this relationship?" Or like the Israelites, do you find yourself saying to God, "I've screwed up, this is how I will love you moving forward." Is that love? Love that is dictated loses something, doesn't it? Perhaps it's time to have a meal with God saying, "God, I've screwed up. I am sorry. It breaks me, how do You want me to love You daily as we move forward together?"

1 John 3:16 says, "By this we know love, that He laid down His life for us, and we ought to lay down our lives for the brothers."

Allow me to close this chapter with a challenge. To know love is to know the sacrificial love of Christ. You and I can never fully understand love–deep, steadfast love–apart from Christ. To know love is to know Christ. I challenge you to spend the next week, three chapters a day, reading the Gospel of John. John, the Casanova of the disciples, wrote an account of Christ's life through the lens of love. Spend a week, three chapters a day, digesting the words. Journal through it on what you notice regarding the steadfast love of Christ. Then at the end of the week, have a meal with God saying, "I've read and have seen love in action. I have a better understanding of Your love. How do you want me to love you in light of what I have seen and know now?" My guess is that what you have learned and how God will ask you to love Him moving forward will not be too different. Give it a try. Be successful in steadfast love towards the King!

INGREDIENT #2: FAITHFULNESS

"Let not steadfast love and faithfulness forsake you;"

"Faithfulness knows no difference between
small and great duties." **John Ruskin**

Faithfulness is easy. Be obedient. Right, easy. Yet daily we fail in our quest to be wholly faithful. This is easy to conceptualize but hard to live out in reality and so we make excuses for ourselves. To a degree, saying "be obedient" is correct. However, faithfulness goes beyond adherence to a set of rules. Do you know anyone living a better life than some Christians in regard to money, position, power, and seemingly live stress-free? Yet, God does not see them as faithful. Know any Christians whom you'd consider a saints, yet they are doing nothing to build the kingdom of God? They act as citizens of Heaven while ignoring the words Christ imparted to us as He physically left the earth. Are they faithful?

There is no shortage of examples of those who are unfaithful from a missional and sinful standpoint. You can argue both are sins, but for our purpose, we must see the distinction as we strive to be biblically successful. Some sin is clear as day: Cheat on your spouse- sin! Tell a blatant lie, not sin! What about not pursuing what ought to be pursued? I am not sinning by sitting in a coffee shop having a cup of coffee, am I? I am if God wants me at the local outreach with my church and I willfully ignore it. Our relationship with God demands that we be faithful to the mission He gave us! Before leaving He stated it clearly, telling us to go into all the world making disciples

(Matthew 28), yet so many of us are not "going!" Our position in the family of God also demands a life of faithfulness. We are children of God: that is our position in the family. Are we living as faithful children of God?

The family unit thrives with faithful living. I have been married for twelve blissful years. I have three kids named after greatness: Landon after Landon, Donavan, Brady, after Tom Brady, and Reagan after Ronald Reagan. Oh, and a black lab named Bruin, after the Boston Bruins! When Ava and I got married, we never imagined the life we'd be living now. It has truly been a roller coaster, but when we promised to be faithful to each other, we meant it: without truly realizing how challenging it would be.

I can be a faithful Dad providing for my kids. But is that complete faithfulness? I can strive to provide for my kids while at the same time neglecting them. How does faithfulness accomplish both? My bookend kids, the oldest and youngest, were in New Hampshire for the week. Brady, my middle son, had to come home early for baseball. I asked him "what is something special you want to do with me that we typically can't do when your brother and sister are home?" He responded, "you know how mom has 'girls' nights?' Can we have a dude's day?" Sure, buddy! Let's do it. Since Fridays are my day off from ministry, we decided to have ourselves a day. I told him we were going to hit the driving range, do some mini-golf, get him an MVP haircut at Sports Clips and get lunch at Buffalo Wild Wings. Full day for sure. When we got to the driving range at 10:30 AM, they told us mini-golf was closed till 1PM for maintenance. Honestly, I was kind of relieved. After we got everything done, it was about 2:45 PM. I was tired. It was my day off. I just wanted to go home. Could I have gone home having been faithful as a Dad to my son? Sure. In this context, I think yes. However, when my son looked at me and said, "Dad, it's after 1 PM, mini-golf to end dude's day?" Every part of me wanted to say no. But I agreed this would be our dude's day and we'd planned for mini golf. I needed to be faithful to the end. So we went mini golfing. I won by 21 strokes. It was a good day.

I can be faithful to Ava by never cheating. Is that true faithfulness? Sure, but is it *full* faithfulness? Yes, I can be faithful by not going outside the relationship and I can be faithful by striving to be a "technically sound" husband, but that is just a part of it. Ava wants me to pursue her. She wants me to be faithful to her alone. She wants me to contribute to the marriage. She wants me to help around the house. She wants me to help with the kids. In all that, I must pursue her. In this way, I am striving to be holy in our relationship and missional in my pursuit of her. Pursuing her is a missional pursuit of LOVE.

What is Biblical success? *Biblical success is when God's heart and God's ways become my heart and my way.* To do this we must be faithful unto God in the manner God desires our faithfulness. God often reminds His people of His faithfulness while asking us to do the same.

Faithfulness: God's Heart and God's Way

Is God always faithful? Yes. Do we always feel that way? No. Wait, can we say that? Can we say that and still be Christians? Yes. It is an honest feeling. Yet, honest feelings are not always truthful feelings. Throughout the Old Testament, God's people lost sight of His faithfulness many times, which led to their unfaithfulness. Sometimes they became demanding, looking for more, neglecting to see God's faithfulness in the moment. Sometimes they forgot the faithfulness of God and wanted to go back to the times in which God proved His faithfulness, (i.e., longing to go back to Egypt). In our broken, fallen nature, we think ourselves more faithful than we are, and we think the faithful One to be less faithful than He is. God is faithful, whether we see it or not.

> **And God spoke all these words, saying, 2 'I am the Lord your God, who brought you out of the land of Egypt, out of the house of slavery. 3 'You shall have no other gods before me' (Exodus 20:1-3).**

> **6 For you are a people holy to the Lord your God. The Lord your God has chosen you to be a people for his treasured possession, out of all the peoples who are on the face of the earth. 7 It was not because you were more in number than any other people that the Lord set his love on you and chose you, for you were the fewest of all peoples, 8 but it is because the Lord loves you and is keeping the oath that he swore to your fathers, that the Lord has brought**

you out with a mighty hand and redeemed you from the house of slavery, from the hand of Pharaoh king of Egypt. 9 Know therefore that the Lord your God is God, the faithful God who keeps covenant and steadfast love with those who love him and keep his commandments, to a thousand generations, 10 and repays to their face those who hate him, by destroying them. He will not be slack with one who hates him. He will repay him to his face. 11 You shall therefore be careful to do the commandment and the statutes and the rules that I command you today (Deuteronomy 7:6-11).

If ever there was a case study on the faithfulness of God, it would be found in God's history with the nation of Israel. God proved not only to be the God of second chances, but also the God of umpteen chances! He sent prophet after prophet, provided judge after judge, and was patient with king after king. Yet, they always turned away. His faithfulness was never enough for them.

God, as per His faithfulness to His people, brings them up out of Egypt with the promise of a land soon to be given to them to enjoy. This is something important–a mark of His faithfulness that He would remind them of. Exodus 20:1 says, "And God spoke all these words: I am the Lord your God who brought you out of Egypt, out of the land of slavery." This is right before giving them the 10 Commandments and insight on how God expected their faithfulness to play out. It was a reminder of what He had done and how He has been faithful. You would think following this God and worshiping Him would be "no big" after He sent those plagues, parted seas, and made it rain food every day. You'd think that, but you would be wrong.

It was just 12 chapters later that the nation's lack of faithfulness hit an all-time high. Moses is up on the mountain getting the rest of God's law. He is getting the needed info from God on how they can properly worship Him. All good things, all good things. Until the people become impatient. "When the people saw that Moses delayed coming down from the mountain, the people gathered themselves together to Aaron and said to him, "Up, make us gods who shall go before us. As for this Moses, the man who brought us up out of the land of Egypt, we do not know what has become of him" (Ex. 32:1). From there they bring together all the gold that God gave them from

Egypt, make a false god and begin to worship it. They go as far as giving credit to this man-made golden calf for bringing them out of Egypt. Again, a calf made with the same gold God gave them when He freed them from bondage! Yet, God is faithful. They paid for their sins, indeed, but eventually, their relatives would be allowed to enter the Promised Land where God once again proved His might.

Those that struggle with faithfulness tend to struggle with forgetfulness. God's people have always been forgetful. They've been forgetful of His promises, what He has done, and what He has commanded. Forgetfulness is not an excuse, it is too easy of a "card" to play. I can't remember my wedding vows word for word, is that an excuse? Nope. My wife can skin a deer and let me know often! Ha! When God's people got to the Promised Land, there was just one thing standing in their way before they could go in and do battle– a raging river at flood level. God sent the priests in, who likely could not swim, but they went in anyway. Faithful. Then the river parts. God's people walk, once again, through parted waters. On the other side, God commanded Joshua to grab 12 stones and make a cairn. Joshua tells the people:

> **20 And those twelve stones, which they took out of the Jordan, Joshua set up at Gilgal. 21 And he said to the people of Israel, "When your children ask their fathers in times to come, 'What do these stones mean?' 22 then you shall let your children know, 'Israel passed over this Jordan on dry ground.' 23 For the Lord your God dried up the waters of the Jordan for you until you passed over, as the Lord your God did to the Red Sea, which he dried up for us until we passed over, 24 so that all the peoples of the earth may know that the hand of the Lord is mighty, that you may fear the Lord your God forever.** Joshua 4:20-24

We need reminders of God's faithfulness. When we set up habits in our lives which help us remember the faithfulness of God, they inspire us to stay faithful. What are cairns in your life? A daily gratitude journal? Dinner at Chili's with your wife year on the anniversary of your first date? The post in your garage with everyone's height and the date on it? The three cairns I have set up in my life to help me remember the faithfulness of God. Two are journals I keep. The first one is a "one line a day" five-year journal. Each day

I write a few thoughts from the day. It helps me track God through the years, enabling me to see His movements in my life. These are things I lose sight of in the moment. The second cairn is an end-of-year journal I keep with my family. Each year on New Year's, or New Year's Eve, we sit down together to think through the year. Years that feel blah, quickly turn into "oh ya, that was fun!" We ask each family member "what was your favorite part of the year?" Then we share longer highlights from each family member. We have been doing it since 2017. And every year, I can declare to you the faithfulness of God. The third cairn is a glass of marbles in my kitchen. At the time of this writing, the one on the right has more marbles than the left. There is a marble for each week we have left with my oldest son till he goes to college. Each week he takes a marble from the right side and puts it on the left side. Then my wife and I pray for wisdom in leading our kids. It's a weekly reminder of how faithful God has been and how much time we have left with our kids under our roof.

As God proves His faithfulness, He demands our faithfulness. He did it with Moses, Joshua, David, and so on. Faithfulness begets faithfulness. Thankfully God is also exceedingly gracious, loving, and merciful, even as our faithfulness fades. Here are the marks of someone successfully faithful before God.

7 Marks of Someone Successful in the Area of Faithfulness

Faithful in Little

This is a fundamental concept, so what complicates it? Our pride. We want to be big-time but we're never willing to put in the time. My son, Landon is a great student. He has never missed a homework assignment to my knowledge. If he tells me his homework is done, I trust him and let him play with his friends. If I can trust you in little things, I can begin to trust in matters of greater significance. Yet, there is an antithesis: if I can't trust you with the little things, why would I trust you with the major things? It is the couple who can't pay their rent but wants me to trust them enough to co-sign on a mortgage. We will go into this in greater depth in chapter 10, but for now, here is a synopsis! In Chapter 10 we will examine Matthew 25:14-23 and find this concept is the thrust of finding success with God. In this passage, Jesus says twice in verses 21 and 23, "His master said to him, 'Well done, good and faithful servant. You have been faithful over a little; I will set you over much. Enter into the joy of your master'.

Have you proven trustworthy with 'little,' proving you can be trusted with much? Do you give 10% of your "little" to advance the kingdom of God or are you waiting for more? Do you give of your time to advance the kingdom of God or are you waiting till you have more time; when the kids get out of the house?

Faith and trust go hand in hand, and that is why I love a percentage-based approach. What would it look like to be able to say to God when it all comes to an end, "God, I always gave you the best of my time with at least 7 hours." How did I get to that number as a base? 168 hours in a week. After subtracting a healthy amount of sleep, you've got 112 hours left. Then remove a reasonable work week, and you are left with 72 hours. 72 hours can be seen as your "flex" time. 7 hours then would be roughly 10% of your time. Legalism is taking what I just said and damning you if you don't do it. No. I simply ask this as a baseline. Can you devote faithfully 7 hours a week to advancing the kingdom of God?

What about percentage-based giving? There was a headline story a few years ago about Jeff Bezos giving $93,000,000. It was a decimal of a percentage of his net worth at the time. Can you imagine if God got a hold of his heart and he gave 10% as a baseline to advance the kingdom of God? Like the attitude of Derek Carr, who in 2017 signed the richest deal in NFL history at that time. A five-year contract for 125 million dollars. At his press conference when asked what he would do with the money he said, "First thing I will do is pay my tithe as I have since I was in college, getting $700 on a scholarship check. That won't change. I'll do that." Percentage-based giving communicates trust better than dollar-amount giving. Bezos is not trusting God when he gives millions, but you giving $300 a month when you make $36,000 a year? That is faithful. That is trust.

Want to know the only time I have ever been audited by the IRS? It was for my giving. They didn't believe it. I had to resubmit the same records I initially submitted and eventually they accepted them. When I give, it does not feel like much in the moment, but at the end of the year, it is one of my favorite numbers to look at because it is something I see God using in my local church. My friend Jordan shared a similar situation. His friend from high school does his taxes. When he showed his giving records, it became a conversation about Jesus! Neither one of us gives thousands at a time. Little gifts throughout the year add up to something that the "professionals" see as unnatural.

In *Call Sign Chaos* by General Jim Mattis, General Mattis speaks to this concept. He says repeatedly in his book, "brilliant in the basics." His point is that in highly stressful situations, if you have not mastered the basics, you will screw up the basics. When you have to think about high-level items and do high-level maneuvers, the basics better come naturally to you or you and others around you may die. One example he gives gripped me. It wasn't a military example, it was a humanitarian example. He spoke about being in the Middle East under President Bush. Some loved our presence and how we were trying to help while others did not. General Mattis said that once a week religious leaders would come together to stir up a revolt. In an already hostile environment, this weekly occurrence escalated the situation. General Mattis said on one such occasion they went into the crowd to hand out water. What? To people trying to kill you? Yup. When it is 110 degrees, it is hard to hate the person giving you free water. At the core of what it means to be a good person, giving someone water on a hot day is a fairly basic action. The army had greater good in mind, but not to the extent of ignoring the good right before them. We must be brilliant in the basics, even the basics of everyday goodness in the face of an enemy.

Stewardship

Type "define stewardship" into Google and here is what pops out: "The job of supervising or taking care of something, such as an organization or property." Merriam -Webster's definition adds, "the careful and responsible management of something entrusted in one's care." By definition, stewardship understands "that which I am stewarding is not my own." It belongs to another; there is written into the definition a chain of command. The steward is the one where "the buck stops with you." For God to be God, He is over all. For our purposes, I'll make certain assumptions that like me, you believe God is all-powerful, in complete control, Creator, and that the whole world belongs to Him, our King. What does the faithful Christian have to give to the One who owns it all? - Faithful stewardship.

In speaking of Apostleship, Paul writes in 1 Corinthians 4:2, "Moreover, it is required of stewards that they be found faithful." A good steward must be seen as faithful. An unfaithful steward will not be seen as good. It's simply counterintuitive. My body belongs to God: will God find me faithful with the care of my body? My financial resources all belong to God: will God find me faithful with the care of my finances? The faithful steward will steward the resources as if the owner was in charge. Do what the owner would do and you will be found faithful.

The Apostle Peter says in 1 Peter 4:10-11, "As each has received a gift, use it to serve one another, as good stewards of God's varied grace: 11 whoever speaks, as one who speaks oracles of God; whoever serves, as one who serves by the strength that God supplies—in order that in everything God may be glorified through Jesus Christ. To him belong glory and dominion forever and ever. Amen." We bring glory to God by living as if He was living our lives. We bring Him glory by making decisions as if He were the one making the decision. What He has given to us, we freely give to others. Why? The faithful Christian is a faithful steward.

Welcomes Intrusion

In today's media-driven world it takes but a moment for "that's none of your business" to become everyone's business. In a moment, what is done in secret can go viral. The facade of faithfulness can be shattered in an instant. Remember that Buffet quote where he said: "It takes 20 years to build a reputation and five minutes to ruin it. If you think about that, you'll do things differently." It took a short Instagram video of a young girl dancing too close to Urban Myer to spiral him out of Jacksonville.

Let's try this. What is the missing word? "Samson and _____." Queue the late-night love song lady Delilah! I grew up a lover, not a fighter and would listen to love songs with Delilah. Yup, Samson and Delilah. This judge of Israel is perhaps best known for his interactions with Delilah. We are introduced to Delilah in Judges 16. There is a small short little verse at the close of Chapter 15 that we so easily brush by. Given what Samson is known for, it is sadly just a footnote to his life. Judges 15 ends by saying, "And he judged Israel in the days of the Philistines twenty years." Maybe Mr. Buffet is on to something! Samson faithfully judged Israel for 20 years. That is a string of 7,300 good days. He had over 175,000 hours of getting it right. Then in a moment, almost as if he got bored with being faithful, he threw it all away by letting someone cut it away.

At some point we will stand before the One who knows it all and there will be NO hiding. In this life we may think we are hiding, but God has a way of bringing to the surface what we thought was buried. So, a characteristic of the faithful Christian is that they *welcome intrusion*. They understand they can welcome accountability because, in the end, we will be held accountable.

In my life, not everyone has access to me. For some, it would feel intrusive if they came to my house, while others don't even have to knock. I've got groups that come to my house often. I have leadership meetings, men's group, church meetings, dinner parties, and so on! They are welcomed downstairs, but it would feel intrusive if they went upstairs to the bedrooms. Who in your life has access to all the areas of your life? Whom do you allow in the front door? Whom do you give the code to your house or the spare key to? Who is allowed to scan through the bedroom closest? It shouldn't be everyone. This is a special spot for a small few you trust, and who have your best interest in mind. Those that don't want to damn you, but to better you- welcome their intrusion.

For me, my wife has full access to my phone, my calendar, and she tracks my location. The location tracking thing is more in her personality. I know personalities are all different, but it really doesn't bother me because I don't feel I have anything to hide. If God sees it all, what is there to hide? The elders of my church have great access to me. They are allowed to speak into my life. I take time to process what they say. Other voices, I have to let bounce off me. There is Pastor Ridder, my pastor, whom I meet with once a month. Nothing is off-limits for him to ask. There is my counselor, with whom it is safe for me to be as open as I can be. Then there are two gentlemen, both elders but elders with deeper access. They have passwords to all my social media, my email, etc. They can look into anything from my "closet" at any time. Why? I don't want to be found faithful for 20 years. I want to be found faithful for a lifetime. We can welcome the intrusive nature of accountability or go viral for all the wrong reasons.

Loyalty

I wake up at 4:12 AM, I come downstairs and drink a glass of water. Then I give my dog some love—don't judge, he's always by my side. Then I turn on a Spotify worship playlist. By this time, my preset coffee is brewed. I make a cup for myself and put out a cup for my wife. Around 4:35AM she strolls down, makes a cup of coffee, and sits across the room from me. As I read a spiritually enriching book, she works through The Bible Recap. After I read, I set out to write 1,000 words. It has become our morning habit. It's calm and peaceful. It is the setting in which I write.

Sitting before me are two examples of loyalty. My dog is a gift. Someone knew the breeder we got him from and gave her money secretively to knock down the price for us. He is a faithful dog. He is by my side. We walk most days down to the bay by my house. He gets legit doggy anxiety when I travel. He is like this for no one else but me. Put him in the middle of me and another and have each of us sprint opposite directions and 10 out of 10 times, he will chase me down. His loyalty, in a season of people crucifying me with their biblical opinion instead of biblical mandates, got me through dark times. He sits directly to my left as I type.

Directly across from me, my wife. Loyalty means the world to her. Her tribe is worth the world—and when people backstab or abandon? Her world is crushed. Her loyalty will bring her to blows with people to defend her family. When I tried leaving my church because it was getting too challenging, her loyalty to God's call helped to keep me in the fight. My wife desires loyalty, but it is not a one-way desire. She is a dispenser of loyalty as well, holding others accountable. She is extreme because she is so passionate about this characteristic. Disloyal people put her in a tailspin: an extreme emotional tailspin.

Jesus is pretty extreme with loyalty as well, He says in Matthew 10:32-33, "So everyone who acknowledges me before men, I also will acknowledge before my Father who is in Heaven, 33 but whoever denies me before men, I also will deny before my Father who is in Heaven." Extreme. In the spiritual sense, a lack of loyalty is a mountain of sin. Jesus wants it all because He gave it all. How can one be faithful if they are occasionally disloyal?

In Matthew 5, Jesus says, if you even look at a woman with lust, you have committed adultery. With my wife directly across from me, she is currently in my focus. She needs to remain there for me to be seen as loyal. I may never physically cheat, but cheating with my eyes? Sin. Not loyal. She wants loyalty in all areas of my life: my mind, my eyes, my body, my speech- all of me. Jesus is just like that. He did not say, love the Lord your God with some of your heart, some of your mind, and some of your soul! He said ALL. He wants all your mind, all your heart, and all your soul. That is love. Your loyalty communicates your faithful love!

God is greater. Then what? Everything. I assume those reading this would agree with such a statement. Want to stay loyal and faithful? Continually find God greater. When another has my focus and I begin to delusionally find them greater, I am on a road to unfaithfulness. There are billions of women out there, loyal faithfulness is seeing the one God has gifted to me as greatness before me. Whenever you are tempted to be unfaithful and disloyal to God, finding Him greater than what is before you will guide you back towards Him.

When it Counts

Faithfulness matters when it counts. Faithfulness is not only being loyal and refusing to exit the marriage, it is fighting for what counts. Faithful people fight. My buddy Doug is a fighter. He wanted me to start this section off with, "The year was 1975 on a September morning, the earth shook while a champion was being birthed…" Yup, he is that guy. Joking aside, I can say I know him to be a man of duty and honor. I have seen this in action. Doug is married with a teenage stepson and a young daughter. He worked on a security team at the local nuclear plant until it began the decommissioning process. Yup, there is a nuclear plant right by me. Weird, people fish right outside of it- yikes! They used to have over 200 security officers: now, they are nearly down to single digits. When Doug was let go, his sense of duty to his family drove him to take any job he could get. He could have sat back, but he bluntly told me, "It does not matter what I am doing; I need to provide for my family."

Doug also owns a few things that go bang-bang. I'm certain that if someone unwelcomed entered his home threatening his family, the neighbors would hear bang-bang. He would not flee. When it counts, he will fight. Sometimes he even fights when it doesn't count, but that is a story for another day!

I have seen him up and leave my men's group study. Why? His stepson was struggling with some stuff and being by his side after seeing the text was more important. It led to a night of driving around looking for his son's deadbeat dad because it meant something to his stepson.

Faithful people need to be faithful when it matters most. If you never provide for your family, why would they see you as faithful? If someone attacks your family and you flee, why would they see you as faithful? If a situation requires your presence and you don't give it, why would they see you as faithful?

Exodus 14:14 says, "The Lord will fight for you, and you have only to be silent." Other translations say, "need only be still." When it matters most, we can trust the One who matters most to spring into action. This is a faithful quality we must live out as well. When it matters most, will we spring into action? James says, "If a brother or sister is poorly clothed and lacking in daily food, and one of you says to them, "Go in peace, be warmed and filled," without giving them the things needed for the body, what good is that?" For real, what good is that? The faithful person springs to action when action is required. When it counts, it will likely cost. Are you willing to give for the betterment of those around you? Ya? That is faithfulness.

Unsafe

Following Christ, from an earthly perspective, is unsafe. We know this, but we do not want to admit it. Was proving His faithfulness to humanity safe for Christ? Was it safe for the apostles? They were martyred. Today, literally, there is a Christian who will die due to his faith in Christ Jesus.

S.D. Gordon, in his book "Quiet Talks on Prayer" likens prayer to a walkie-talkie. He says that for the Christian, prayer is like having a walkie-talkie on the front lines, phoning back to home base to bring the reinforcements. Why are more Christians not sold out in prayer? Perhaps because they are not on the front lines. Those on the front lines know the intense need and benefits communication provides.

The devil loves safe. The devil loves comfort. In 2018, Craig Groeschel tweeted, "Find comfort in being uncomfortable. Growth and comfort never coexist. If something doesn't challenge you, it won't change you." The devil loves the facade of safety and comfort because ultimately, it prevents us from being faithful Christians, and from accomplishing anything worthwhile. "He faithfully eats twinkies each day" vs. "She faithfully serves the underprivileged." Huge difference in our understanding of faithfulness. Both statements describe faithfulness. Only one though honors God and lends itself to a life of purpose.

This is where the Christian way directly opposes the American way. We want our comfort. We want safety. Ok, fine. I'll be reckless and play Russian Roulette to prove my faithfulness. No, God gave you a brain. Use it. Understand though as you exercise your faith and your brain, plan on finding yourself in some very unsafe situations.

Noah built a boat for a surge of water.
Moses confronted the most powerful man on earth.
The Israelites walked through a parted sea.
Abraham nearly sacrificed his son.
Stephen was stoned.
The early church was persecuted.
Paul was beaten, jailed, and killed.
Jesus died on the cross.

Yet, giving 10% is not for us. Allotting 7 hours a week is too much. Moving my family to take a job God asks me to take is too much. Leaving the penthouse to help those stuck in the outhouse, nah. Playing it safe is just a nice way of saying I don't want to sacrifice.

Jesus said in Luke 9:23-25, "And he said to all, "If anyone would come after me, let him deny himself and take up his cross daily and follow me. 24 For whoever would save his life will lose it, but whoever loses his life for my sake will save it. 25 For what does it profit a man if he gains the whole world and loses or forfeits himself?""

Why do we think Jesus was kidding? Deny myself. Take up my cross. How often? Daily. Practice something daily and you will find the faithful life. Jesus did not die for you to live a safe life, He died to give you a safe eternity. The pathway? Self-denial. Death. Hardship. Stop playing it safe and begin living the faithful life Christ exemplified for us.

"And behold, I am with you always, to the end of the age." (Matthew 28:20B). You don't do this alone. You walk through the hardship and the minefield of this life with Christ by your side. Push all your chips to the middle of the table and go all in.

"And he returned from following him and took the yoke of oxen and sacrificed them and boiled their flesh with the yokes of the oxen and gave it to the people, and they ate. Then he arose and went after Elijah and assisted him." (1 Kings 19:20)

Elijah calls Elisha to follow him. Elisha does. How? By destroying the family business. This was his livelihood. This was the fallback plan if the whole Elijah thing did not work out. He had nothing to turn back to and he eliminated all his options except one- the call of God on his life. This is reckless abandonment. This is unsafe. This is faithfulness.

Initiative

The faithful Christian must know a life of "going." Is there a time to wait on the Lord? Of course. Every 7 days we are to stop going and simply be. The unfaithful Christian is "being" 6 days a week and "going" 1. As Jesus ascends to Heaven, what is His first command? After reminding the disciples of His authority, he says, "Go, therefore..." So, we must go. We must get off the couch. We must go to our neighbor. We must go help the lowly. Go help the widow. For God's literal sake, we must get back to being a people marked by "going."

Make cookies for your neighbor.

Serve at a soup kitchen.

Sponsor a Compassion child.

Go to church.

Speak up for the marginalized.

Go on a mission trip.

> **19 But Jews came from Antioch and Iconium, and having persuaded the crowds, they stoned Paul and dragged him out of the city, supposing that he was dead. 20 But when the disciples gathered about him, he rose up and entered the city, and on the next day he went on with Barnabas to Derbe.** Acts 14:19-20

Paul has just started as a missionary. He's still learning and getting the hang of this whole "share Jesus and start churches" thing. He is in Lystra and finds himself among some bad dudes. They try to kill him. In fact, they thought they had. They drag his assumed dead body outside the city and leave it there. You already read the verse, so you know what Paul does, but pause for a second and think, what would you have done? This homeboy? I am heading for the hills. I would get on my donkey and high tail it out of there. If I thought about trying to act brave, I'd plan to walk in and go all Rambo on them. I would certainly not get back up to preach the same message that nearly got me killed.

Paul did.

That's initiative.

The best part? Many of them came to faith in Jesus Christ.

Faithful Christians take initiative.

The Example of Jesus

Jesus is the quintessential example of faithfulness. Books could be written on the faithfulness of Christ. Is He faithful to keep His promises? Yes. Is He standing before God, faithful in our defense? Yes. Yet, I want to narrow our focus to His faithful endurance. Jesus was faithful in His obedience to the Father in completing the task that was set before Him.

> **Have this mind among yourselves, which is yours in Christ Jesus, 6 who, though he was in the form of God, did not count equality with God a thing to be grasped, 7 but emptied himself, by taking the form of a servant, being born in the likeness of men.8 And being found in human form, he humbled himself by becoming obedient to the point of death, even death on a cross. 9 Therefore God has highly exalted him and bestowed on him the name that is above every name, 10 so that at the name of Jesus every knee should bow, in Heaven and on earth and under the earth, 11 and every tongue confess that Jesus Christ is Lord, to the glory of God the Father.** Philippians 2:5-11

Jesus was faithful amid hostility. I wonder if it was the example of Christ that got Paul stoned and left for dead outside of Lystra, to get up and go back into the city. Christ, the embodiment of love was hated. Think about that. There has never been a greater example of a life marked by love. Ever. Jesus Christ is the truest and best example we have of a loving life. Yet, He was hated. They spat on Him. They punched Him. They whipped Him. They insulted Him. They made fun of His mother. They convicted Him. They treated Him as a criminal. They twisted His words. They put nails through His arms and feet. They hung Him naked. They mocked Him. Could we maintain the same faithful love in such hostility?

> **Therefore, since we are surrounded by so great a cloud of witnesses, let us also lay aside every weight, and sin which clings so closely, and let us run with endurance the race that is set before us, 2 looking to Jesus, the founder and perfecter of our faith, who for the joy that was set before him endured the cross, despising the shame, and is seated at the right hand of the throne of God. 3**

Consider him who endured from sinners such hostility against himself, so that you may not grow weary or fainthearted. Hebrews 12:1-3

Jesus faithfully endured the cross with joy. It should go without saying, but there was nothing enjoyable about the cross. In modern times, we could liken it to an electric chair. What would it be like to have a relative who was convicted, then sentenced, and finally executed via the electric chair? Wouldn't that be a black eye for the family? Wouldn't that be a source of shame? Yet, it is this type of trial that Christ endured for you and me. Yet, he did so with a positive attitude. Could we be so faithful through our hardships, with such an attitude?

In faithful obedience, Jesus maintained a humble Spirit. This is not me. If there is a faithful example that would convict me to my core, it is this one. I want people to know my sacrifice. I want people to know when I wake up to prepare sermons. I want people to see the sacrifice and the toll ministry takes on my family. I want them to know when I have 5-6 evening meetings. I want them to know about my 60-hour work weeks. Why? I feel elevated. Why? I am sinful. Jesus left the comforts of Heaven. In light of what Jesus left behind, you could say His entire life was work. Jesus worked 24/7 in that regard. I'm still living, so I've not yet given my life to this cause. Jesus did. Jesus served those who would complain about sacrifice to His face! Jesus served those who returned His love with hate. If anyone had room to be served, it was Jesus. But as He said, He came to serve. When you read Philippians 2, then consider all that Jesus said and didn't say; there was no one more humble than Jesus. In humility, as He is dying on the cross, what is His concern? Others. As He was praying, He asked for the cup to pass Him, but He was also focused on His disciples and those to come (US!). Can we be faithfully sacrificial with such a humble attitude?

39 And going a little farther He fell on his face and prayed, saying, "My Father, if it be possible, let this cup pass from me; nevertheless, not as I will, but as you will." Matthew 26:39

42 Again, for the second time, He went away and prayed, "My Father, if this cannot pass unless I drink it, your will be done." Matthew 26:42

Jesus faithfully placed God's will over His own. Obedience can be easy. Some of the tasks my wife asks me to do that I grumble about are honestly not that tough. Some of the things I ask of my kids, despite their attitude, are not that tough. Faithfulness transcends the easy and the desirable. Jesus asks God to find another way with an attitude resolved to obey. He is resolved not to do what He wants, He is determined to do what the Father wants. Jesus was willing to obey against His desires. You can't sincerely pray for God's will while resolved to go your own way. Jesus placed God's will over His own. God has given us free will, and because of this, faithfulness will always test our will. Who is God? A great litmus test to that question: whose will has the upper hand in your life? Elizabeth Elliot is credited with saying, "To pray, 'thy will be done,' I must be willing, if that answer requires it, that my will be undone." Will we faithfully let the will of God be the most essential thing in our lives?

What is Biblical success? *Biblical success is when God's heart and God's ways become my heart and my way.* Want to be successful in the eyes of God? Be a person characterized by faithfulness.

INGREDIENT #2: FAITHFULNESS
BIBLICAL CASE STUDY

"Let not steadfast love
and faithfulness forsake you;" (Proverbs 3:3)

"Well done is better than well said." **Tom Brady, Sr.**

Biblical success is when God's ways and God's heart become my way and my heart. When my life crosses that final finish line, I do not hope to hear, "Well done, good and *successful* servant." I have never dreamed of hearing those words from God Almighty. I live like I'm striving to hear those words though. So what do I dream of hearing? "Well done, good and faithful servant." Lord Jesus, this is indeed what I strive to hear.

At the start of 2022, a wave of motivation came over my wife and I. I've already mentioned or alluded to our morning habits when talking about my wife. These new habits are something we very much enjoy. Again, as I type this, she sits across from me, and the song "I belong to Jesus" by Bethel Music is lightly playing in the background. We are up at 4:20 AM and reading, journaling, and writing by 4:30 AM. We do this for about 90 minutes. It is peaceful and tranquil.

About five days into this newly formed habit, which we love, an interruption started waking up around 5:30 AM. The interruption has a name, Landon Coache, my oldest son. He sets his own alarm. He does not have to wake up till 6:15 AM but likes waking up early to move at his own pace. His younger brother likes moving at his own pace but doesn't plan the extra time, but that is a story for another day ha! Landon wakes up, comes downstairs, and lays on the couch, abruptly "interrupting" our peaceful environment. He starts asking innocent and natural questions—no big deal. But, given five days of a habit formed before he went back to school, I was very annoyed. It is here I was very convicted.

I want my son to know what a faithful life looks like, naturally and organically. I didn't set his alarm so he could come downstairs and watch mom and dad. He did. And thus he gets an unforced snapshot into our lives. He knows my goals: I've read them to him. He knows I'm focused on accomplishing big things this year, so he gets to see that "well done is better than well said." I want to be the parent my kids can look back and talk about in regards to faithful living. I don't want them to talk about a 'good life,' but about a family that lived out true authentic faith in Jesus: a family where life was not dominated by self, but was all about Jesus. I want them to see we lived the full life and it wasn't a dull life.

What do you want others to naturally see from you? What would it look like if God's people truly, individually and collectively, were obsessed with the faithful life? What would it look like if we were obsessed with the glory of God shining through us? What would it look like to have two decisions before us that are both excellent? Only one brings God's glory, so we say, "welp it's decided! Whatever will bring my God glory, that is what I will do." What would it look like to live a faithful life, not just a few faithful moments?

In this case study, I want to look at a guy named Daniel. He is living in a land, Babylon, that is anything but supportive of his Christian faith. As an exile from Israel, now living in this foreign land, Daniel has seen some stuff and has been around the block. As we unpack this story, Daniel is around 80 years old. They didn't have the medical advancements we have today, so we can say that culturally, Daniel was old as dirt!

> **Then this Daniel became distinguished above all the other high officials and satraps, because an excellent spirit was in him. And the king planned to set him over the whole kingdom.** Daniel 6:3

All the local leaders have come together. These are the wise men of the land. They all hold positions and are equally accountable to the king. Around 120 of them gathered, and Daniel has become a standout. He is a cut above the rest. He has an extraordinary spirit, he is wise, has insight, and is intelligent. What was the result? The king wants to put him in charge of the land, meaning all present would be subject to him. Everyone loves it, no? No. Success has a way of multiplying your enemies.

> **Then the high officials and the satraps sought to find a ground for complaint against Daniel with regard to the kingdom, but they could find no ground for complaint or any fault, because he was faithful, and no error or fault was found in him.** Daniel 6:4

Jealousy is powerful. Left unchecked it translates into some of the darkest hatred. People hate his character. They search, but they cannot find fault or corruption in him. They cannot find negligence. He is trustworthy. If you're Daniel, despite the fact that you are about to be backstabbed, this is a huge spiritual compliment! So what do you do when you can't find fault with someone? You start scheming, of course!

> **Then these men said, "We shall not find any ground for complaint against this Daniel unless we find it in connection with the law of his God."** Daniel 6:5

What a testimony to Daniel! If we can count on anything, we can count on Daniel to be the man of God we know him to be! If it comes to choosing the law of the land or the law of God, we can count on him picking God. Why? His faithful reputation preceded him.

So these officials go to the king and blow a ton of smoke up his butt. Fun fact, blowing smoke up the butt was a common medical procedure in the late 1700's and is where we get this phrase. Weird. So after stroking the king's ego, they 'suggest' to him that he put a law in motion. The law being, for thirty days no one in the land can make a petition of another god or person. All petitions for thirty days must go before the king, otherwise be thrown into the lion's den. They know what Daniel will do. Cancel culture has come knocking on Daniel's door. To me, this sounds wildly exhausting. But the king is new and is trying to establish his throne. He does not know he is being played; why would he? It is a power move playing to the king's ego. It works. He signs this into law. Daniel should be retiring but finds himself in the middle of political games.

I had a small retirement party for Wheels and Sue Langworthy a few weeks back. They are dear friends. We consider them family. "Ya, cool friends, did you say his name is Wheels?" Ya, it's actually Robert, but few know it. When he came to Jesus, he started working in the youth ministry at his church. The youth pastor said, "I need a wheelman." So Robert, in his newfound faith, stepped up and became the bus driver. He's been Wheels ever since.

Before Wheels, Robert was in that drugs and alcohol life. This life got him locked up in the dungeons of NYC for a few nights. After rehab, he found Jesus. In finding Jesus, he found true life and has never been the same. Robert probably dreamed of retiring boozing and cruising, but that was Robert. He died. Wheels, the most faithful Christian I know, is alive in Christ. So this retirement party was his fellow elders and a few key people from our church. It was simple. Few nice words, subs, a few gifts, and then we prayed for our church. Then, like a jerk, he left for nine months to travel the country. He's not a jerk. He's a brother. I love him. I'm still bitter, ha!

Like I said, to me, Wheels defines a faithful Christian. If there is a Daniel in my life, it is Wheels. He's traveling the country in retirement with his amazing wife. I know he's praying for me. I know he's going to meet people. I know there will be people all over the country that come to faith in Jesus because they met Jesus through Wheels. One of the gifts we got him was a Yeti mug that says, "Well done good and faithful servant." Yup. Truth. If there is anyone I know where you would need to somehow use his faith to trap him, it is Wheels Langworthy. His faith makes him predictable. If Wheels were left to choose between his God and honestly anything else, God would win 100% of the time. Ok, he's not perfect. So maybe 95% of the time!

As we think about a faithful reputation, could someone play our faith for personal gain? It's an interesting question. Yes? How would they do it? No? What are the current struggles they could bring up to bring us down? If we were rising in power, would people have to play political games as these dirtbags did to Daniel? Or, with enough digging, would it be easy to take us out? "Oh, you want to promote _____? last week he…" Or, "You're giving the project to _____? Check out this text and what he really thinks about you."

Back to our story, with the law newly signed, what would Daniel do? Would the faithful reputation translate to faithful actions?

> **When Daniel knew that the document had been signed, he went to his house where he had windows in his upper chamber open toward Jerusalem. He got down on his knees three times a day and prayed and gave thanks before his God, as he had done previously.** Daniel 6:10

Daniel wastes no time obeying his God. He is completely unfazed. He keeps on keeping on. He never pauses to ponder, "what will this cost me?" The faithless are concerned with what the situation before them will cost them. The faithful? They have already counted the cost of following Jesus and have determined He is worth it no matter the cost. The faithful have determined Jesus to be priceless! Their banner is "you can have all this world, just give me Jesus!"

So Daniel did what he had always done. Nothing public about his defiance. No public statement. No grandstanding on social media. He is simply honoring God, unwilling to hide. He could have taken a month off. After all, it's only a month. He could have hidden and gone into a private room. Is that what the faithful do? Not in Daniel's mind. Instead, they pinned him against the king of the land and the King of Kings. At the end of the day, Daniel is faithful to the king of the land only when it does not interfere with faithfulness to the true King. His heavenly King is the priority. Always.

Daniel's faithfulness made him predictable. These dirtbags knew where to look. They knew where to find him. They knew what they would find. They did; they found a faithful man maintaining his faithful walk. Once caught, these dirtbags go to the king of the land like whiny first graders. They remind the king of what he had said; the law he put into place. Then they inform him of what Daniel has done.

> **Then the king, when he heard these words, was much distressed and set his mind to deliver Daniel. And he labored till the sun went down to rescue him.** Daniel 6:14

The king is pacing in distress. This is a mess. Will delaying keep the inevitable from happening? Nope, these sleazeballs come back hellbent on killing Daniel. They remind the king that even he is subject to the laws of the land. He is bound to his own words. The king knows this is a case of entrapment, but the trap worked. They used his ego, his pride, and his power against him. Even his absolute power as the king could not get Daniel out of trouble. So, with that, he condemns Daniel to the lion's den, saying…

> **The king declared to Daniel, "May your God, whom you serve continually, deliver you!"** Daniel 6:16B

He sends Daniel away, hoping his petitions to the One true King would work. He is now looking to Daniel's faithful King to bring about deliverance. The king is beside himself and "hanging on a prayer." But Daniel? The one who has been faithful in prayer? He's seemingly unfazed. He's simply obedient and faithful, taking it all in stride. Faithfulness in prayer has a calming effect on the faithful.

So they throw him in. They place a stone over the den. Why? They want to ensure this 80-year-old geriatric wouldn't go Rambo on the lions and climb out of the den. For us? It is a reminder that there is no earthly hope for deliverance. Thus why the king goes sleepless and won't eat. He's presumably praying or at least taking the religious posture through fasting. This is destroying him. He is in agony. His friend is in a "hopeless" den. His fake friends celebrate what is a sure death.

Reading between the lines, it is Daniel who is at peace. We only get a snapshot of the king's emotions. The following day, Daniel says, "all good in the hood" of sorts. So with some assumptions, the dirtbags? Celebratory. Seems like they have won. The king? Agony. Daniel? Peaceful, as all is good. He is likely sleeping just fine! Being untrue to his God was never an option. He is fine with how this all played out. There is no conforming for the transformed.

In 1951, social psychologist Solomon Asch conducted a study known as the "line test." You can google "Asch line test" and find images. He wanted to see if he could get people to answer a very obvious question incorrectly just by adding some social pressure. So in his comparable group, he gave people a question to answer with no outside influences. The question had to be really obvious. Participants had to decide which line was the same size. On the left side was a single line. On the right side were three options, all different sizes. One of those lines was obviously the same size as the line on the right side. 99% of participants got it correct. The question had an obvious answer.

Then, Asch had participants put in a room with seven confederates (social actors). They knew the test and had already determined how they would answer. The intention was that they would answer first, giving a wrong answer and stating their thoughts. Then, last, would be the clueless subject. The findings? Asch could get about 75% of participants to conform at some point. Only 25% of participants never conformed at any point! Remember, this was an obvious test that 99% of participants answered correctly without any pressure!

The participants should have been confident. They should have said, "I know the answer is A, forget what y'all are saying, you're tripping. It's A." But like all humans, when pressure from our peers comes, we, by nature, conform. What faithful decision, right now, do you know is the right decision? Where could you perceive future pressure? What decision do you need to lock in based on your current faithful walk with Jesus? What do you need to decide now in order to stay faithful tomorrow? The unfaithful ponder, while the faithful are predetermined.

When he says love should bring you to bed, what has your faithfulness predetermined? When your boss says to fudge the numbers to land the deal, what has your faithfulness predetermined? When your best friend needs answers to a test so he doesn't flunk for the year, what has your faithfulness predetermined? When you find yourself with an influx of money, what has your faithfulness predetermined?

As you think of the future you, is the future you willing to get "canceled" for the cause of Christ? Christian character is not formed in the moment of adversity. Christian character is revealed in the moment of adversity. What character is about to be revealed in the future moments coming your way? It worked out just fine for Daniel. At daybreak, the king goes to see if things are all good with Daniel...

> **As he came near to the den where Daniel was, he cried out in a tone of anguish. The king declared to Daniel, "O Daniel, servant of the living God, has your God, whom you serve continually, been able to deliver you from the lions?" Then Daniel said to the king, "O king, live forever! My God sent his angel and shut the lions' mouths, & they have not harmed me, because I was found blameless before him; & also before you, O king, I have done no harm."** Daniel 6:20-22

These are the only words in the entire narrative that Daniel speaks. His faithful life has done all the talking. He uses his life and words to direct all who would hear to the glory of God. The faithful in Christ live lives proclaiming Christ.

The king orders Daniel to get pulled out. He is examined. All is true! No harm has been done to him because he trusted in God. Trust in the Lord is what precipitated a faithful walk. So, with his faithful walk, Daniel had an angel and lions staring at him all night. Those that lacked faith? Those dirtbags? They and their families are thrown into the lion's den and eaten before hitting the ground. Do you blame the lions? They just had to stare at their snack all night, unable to eat him. They were certainly *hangry*! Please note that this is a narrative and not an absolute. Sometimes, the faithful are eaten. See the early church for plenty of examples. In chapter 6, we will examine three young men with this understanding: God can, but we will not presume God will.

As for King Darius, he, in his own way "blogs" about the experience...

> **Then King Darius wrote to all the peoples, nations, and languages that dwell in all the earth: "Peace be multiplied to you. I make a decree, that in all my royal dominion people are to tremble and fear before the God of Daniel, for he is the living God, enduring forever;**

his kingdom shall never be destroyed, & his dominion shall be to the end. He delivers and rescues; he works signs and wonders in heaven and on earth, he who has saved Daniel from the power of the lions." So this Daniel prospered during the reign of Darius and the reign of Cyrus the Persian. Daniel 6:25-28

The king, now with awe for God, sends God viral! All people are to fear and tremble. All people are to understand the magnitude and might of Daniel's God. The miraculous deliverance of Daniel clearly impacted King Darius. In the king's statement, we learn what he has learned. He has a new, healthy, and fresh respect for the One True King!

His declaration accomplishes two purposes. First, it recognizes the greatness and superiority of Israel's God. It acknowledges their God has no rivals. This is huge coming from the king of one of the most powerful nations on earth. Secondly, it cancels out the stupid edict previously declared to trap Daniel and the king. Daniel's testimony and faithfulness sure had an impact. Instead of fearing lions, fear the Lord. Do so with awe and wonder!

This a question we may or may not think to ask ourselves, but it is critical to ask: what is meant by fear? First, let me paint a picture of how I handle "fear" in my house. It is the difference between allowing fear to *control* or respect to *guide*.

Okay, so one of my boys needed that birds and the bees talk the other night. Lots of fun. Tell your boy to tell you everything they have heard, all the words, knowing they cannot get into trouble, and you will hear it all! Within thirty seconds, we are both blushing. As we talked about life, offering him our worldview on things he had already heard a little about, I had a decision to make; do I scare him into holiness or guide him towards holiness?

When he mentioned smoking, I could show him a picture of a black lung and express the dangers. Fear driven. Or I could remind him that our bodies are a gift and that we treat them well out of respect for God. This is glory driven. When he mentioned drinking and drugs, I could show him pictures of a drunk driver or one of those commercials from 'back in the day' with the slogan, "this is your brain on drugs, any questions?" Fear driven. Or I could remind him that God asks us to respect the laws of the land and to always be in control of our bodies. Glory driven. When he mentions sex, I could talk to him about the hardships of having a child and caring for a child. Fear driven. Or I could remind him that God asks us to keep the marriage bed pure and that the institution of marriage is best suited to handle the challenges that come with having a child. Glory driven.

As a parent, I want my kids to fall so in love with Jesus that disrespecting Him becomes unthinkable. I want that personally. I want to be so obsessed with love for God that the thought of disappointing Him is inconceivable. This is a quality that is critical in a faithful relationship. So, naturally, doesn't my wife want this to be true? Where I'm so obsessed with my love for her that the thought of disappointing her is unthinkable? This motivates faithfulness. If this is overwhelming in my life, for God and my wife, it can, and perhaps should, become *a point of fear.*

Do I fear disappointing my wife? Do I fear disappointing God? Could such fear drive faithfulness? In the passage, we just looked at how fear is mentioned, specifically fear and trembling. The unsaved, yes, fear and tremble. There ought to be deep fear of an eternity apart from Christ. However, for the Christian? 1 John 4:18 reminds us that Christ's perfect love casts out fear. So is there relational fear in our relationship with God? The love of Christ that took the penalty of sin away, removing the fear of punishment. We do not fear eternal damnation. PRAISE GOD! Relationally, a transcendent fear is still in play. Fear that may best be seen in an old fuddy-duddy word; reverence. Google defines reverence as "a deep respect for someone or something." Based on my deep respect, my reverent fear drives my faithfulness to God. The Christian understands fear much differently than how the rest of the world should understand it. I'm not obsessed with fear. I'm obsessed with God's glory to the point that I fear the thought of not bringing Him glory. May my life be a story of God's glory. May all I do and say put God's glory on full send!

Here is what we learn in this story and through Daniel's example: ***The faithful live a story of God's glory!***

January 2021 was particularly challenging for my family. In the introduction, I opened up about my challenges as a Christian and pastor. Then came the call that caused time to stand still. My parents called me and said my 14-month precious niece had passed away suddenly. It was devastating not only for my brother and his wife but personally for me as well. Sparing all the details, I can tell you that week, I saw faithfulness in action. While their pastor was sitting with the whole family in their living room, my sister-in-law responded to this question, "what do you want to be said at the funeral?" How she responded has stuck with me. She instantly and boldly proclaimed, "You preach Jesus because that is the only way any of this makes sense." A few days later, sitting behind my brother and sister-in-law, I saw them with raised hands shouting through sobs, "It is well with my soul." Character was not formed, it was revealed. Faithful.

Fast forward a few weeks. Before the situation with my brother, it was recommended that I seek counsel from someone who has suffered loss. As a pastor, 2020 brought loss in many different ways. I set up a meeting with Lenny Schmidt. It was postponed a week or two conveniently after my niece's funeral.

Lenny, about seven months prior, was diagnosed with pancreatic cancer. Within a month of his diagnosis, his new wife received news that she had brain cancer. Both of them, already familiar with loss, were in late stages. She was new to the Christian faith. I remember the elders coming together to pray for Lenny. He asked us to pray that he would outlive his wife so he could take care of her. She was new to the faith, and he wanted to be around to be physically and spiritually strong to support her through this. God said yes to his prayer.

At my meeting with Lenny, he gave me tremendous advice for which I am forever thankful. He also gave me a blank check, signed, saying, "be a blessing to your brother." His faithfulness was exemplified in his generosity.

At the close of 2021, having outlived his wife, Lenny's life drew to a close. Mid-December, my executive pastor and I went to visit Lenny at his home. Lenny was a top giver in my church. Driving up, what were we to expect? A mansion? A nice car in the driveway with some guy named Biff polishing it? Nope. He lived with his son. I don't think he owned a car in the closing years of his life. Rather, I saw him in a hospice-provided bed in the living room facing the TV. He was surrounded by family. Family all walking with Jesus. Above the TV was a sign that said, "As for me and my house, we will serve the Lord."

This exemplified a faithful Christian. The faithful life? Lenny had scars not cars. Today you won't find Lenny's former mansion because Lenny lived for the mansion of tomorrow, his eternal home. He was not ultimately healed here but he was content in Christ's eternal healing. He lived a faithful life, the end proved it.

When it all comes to an end, will your life be a story of God's glory? Will it be a story that never allowed circumstances to dictate life? When you cross that final finish line, will you have lived a life obsessed with the glory of God? When there is a decision before you, will you pick the one that brings God the most glory? Learn to do this consistently and you will live the faithful life. You will find success as you hear, "well done, good and faithful servant" from the Lord of Lords and King of Kings.

INGREDIENT #3: COMMITMENT

"Let not steadfast love and faithfulness
forsake you; bind them around your neck" (Proverbs 3:3)

"You need to make a commitment, and once you make it,
then life will give you some answers." **Les Brown**

Commitment. A word easily declared but hardly lived out. When Christ spoke of commitment, He spoke in all-or-nothing terms. Humanity, this has always been our struggle has it not? We have moments of being all in, followed by moments of great failure. Is this why most of us relate with the Apostle Peter? One moment declaring he would die for Christ, boldly saying all could fall away but he would not. Then, mere moments later, he denies even knowing Christ. We can relate. No one else committed to getting out of the boat when Jesus was walking toward them. Peter did. Committed. Then, sees the storm and begins to lack faith. Lacking faith leads to sinking commitment. This is going to be a challenging chapter because we all lack from time to time.

Paul, very much an all-or-nothing type guy, struggled with this as well. He said in Romans, *"So now it is no longer I who do it, but sin that dwells within me.* ***18*** *For I know that nothing good dwells in me, that is, in my flesh. For I have the desire to do what is right, but not the ability to carry it out.* ***19*** *For I do not do the good I want, but the evil I do not want is what I keep on doing.* ***20*** *Now if I do what I do not want, it is no longer I who do it, but sin that dwells within me."* (Romans 7:17-20). Paul was committed. Yet he struggled. There is a danger when we stop struggling, when we stop leaning into grace. When we stop leaning into the process of progress, we must commit to the struggle.

From an earthly standpoint, I have a strong commitment to three relationships: my wife, kids, and church. When Ava and I said our "I do's," we committed ourselves to each other. Commitment in this relationship eliminates many questions I used to ask. Questions that if I were still asking would drive me to the "questionable." I'm committed to Ava, so I don't need to ask what _____ (girl's name, not my wife) is doing on Friday night. I do not need to ask if another likes my outfit, I ask if Ava does. Should I spend time with Ava or _____ (girl's name)? Not a question. If these things were questions, would Ava feel my commitment? I can pick her over and over again, but if I live in a state of questioning, would she feel my commitment? My commitment to her eliminates the questions keeping me from the questionable.

My relationship with my kids is a different type of commitment. They did not pick me. They had no choice in the matter. Ava and I made three choices known now as Landon, Brady, and Reagan. This could be said of my wife as well, but how do I learn commitment through my kids? By trying. By growing. I just googled "books on parenting." Here is a cut and paste: "About 186,000,000 results (0.85 seconds)." Doubtful that all represents an actual book, but far-fetched to think we could read all the books on parenting. Read books for sure, there is wisdom there. However, reading and doing are worlds apart. My point I can know, so I think, how to be a great parent. This does not mean I am a great parent. Landon is my firstborn. As first, he is perpetually first. I am always learning with him. Am I committed to being a better Dad for him? Am I committed to admitting my wrongs? If not, I will lose my son. Am I committed to spending time with him? Dieter Uchtodrf said, "In family relationships, 'love' is really spelled 't-i-m-e,' time." The best way my kids will experience my commitment to them is by spending time with them and my commitment to growing as a Dad.

My church has taught me commitment. My church has taught me that I am committed to joyous pain. Twice I have tried quitting. Once on a prayer walk with God. The other time, I submitted my resignation to the elder team. Both were rejected. I thought when I committed to starting a church that I was committing to hard work and with great results. That was the case at first. Tit for tat commitment. Then pain. People leave. People say things. The church is used in political games. Panic attacks. Pressure. Stress. I have had two panic attacks now in the five years at my current church. Once in the shower as I was getting ready to head over to sign our first lease on our current building. The second? Late May of 2020 when then President Trump demanded that states allow churches to open back up. I had already been roasted by people on both sides of the aisle, and then felt like I was just thrown into another political fight. What does this have to do with commitment? It would be so easy to leave my church. It is a different relationship than what I have with my family. Although, in many ways it is harder, staying in it is a commitment to calling. At the end of the day, that is the lesson for me through my church. I am committed to Christ through them. They are simply a byproduct of my commitment to Jesus. If Christ tells me to stay, I will. If He tells me to leave, I will. They are a byproduct of obedience, testing my commitment to Christ.

All these lessons could be summed up in one offshoot of commitment: holiness. There is much in life I can commit myself to as I commit myself to the Lord. Do I commit myself to relationships, tasks, and habits that make me holier? Holy as Christ defines holy? Does it put me in pursuit of the lost unbelieving world? Does it have me investing in fellow Christians to see their growth? As I commit to my wife, family and church, am I holier? Am I more like Christ? Is there holy progress to a holier life? Am I committed to being better by committing to what is better? Think about everything vying for your commitment, you can't commit to it all. To try to commit to everything is to commit to nothing. You must choose. Commitment to one great thing will require 1,000 no's to many good things. There are many good women, kids and churches out there. I'm committed to my great Ava, to some great kids named Landon, Brady and Reagan and a great church called Wellspring.

What is Biblical success? *Biblical success is when God's heart and God's ways become my heart and my way.* To do this, we must be committed to God in the manner God desires for us to be committed. Too often we see ourselves as more committed than we are in actuality. Why? We've made the comparable the world far from God rather than His Son Jesus!

Commitment: God's Heart and God's Way

At the end of the chapter, we will look to Christ to see how He exemplified a committed life. Here, we want to examine one of His teachings on a committed life. It is a hard teaching. Brace yourselves. Be open to correction. On this side of Heaven, no one can read this passage without identifying an area where they ought to be giving God more of themselves. Here is what Christ, the Holy Son of God, completely committed to obeying the Father said;

> **25 Now great crowds accompanied him, and he turned and said to them, 26 "If anyone comes to me and does not hate his own father and mother and wife and children and brothers and sisters, yes, and even his own life, he cannot be my disciple. 27 Whoever does not bear his own cross and come after me cannot be my disciple. 28 For which of you, desiring to build a tower, does not first sit down and count the cost, whether he has enough to complete it? 29 Otherwise, when he has laid a foundation and is not able to finish, all who see it begin to mock him, 30 saying, 'This man began to build and was not able to finish.' 31 Or what king, going out to encounter another king in war, will not sit down first and deliberate whether he is able with ten thousand to meet him who comes against him with twenty thousand? 32 And if not, while the other is yet a great way off, he sends a delegation and asks for terms of peace. 33 So, therefore, any one of you who does not renounce all that he has cannot be my disciple. 34 "Salt is good, but if salt has lost its taste, how shall its saltiness be restored? 35 It is of no use either for the soil or for the manure pile. It is thrown away. He who has ears to hear, let him hear." Luke 14:25-35**

Followers go hard, fans peace out. A follow is better than a like. Jesus isn't looking for views, He's looking for subscribers. Do you get what I am throwing down? There is this huge crowd following Jesus. They are following Him in proximity and not reality. Jesus has a big crowd. In our world, He's getting all the views and likes a person could hope for. Some are even buying His merch! But Jesus turns to them and essentially says, "I don't want your views, I want you to subscribe. I don't want your likes, I want you to follow." Come on Jesus, isn't this good enough? No, more shows commitment and He wants more. Jesus doesn't want us counted in the crowd's numbers, He wants us counted among those actually following, chasing, and desiring to be like Him. Jesus doesn't hold back. Jesus doesn't care to keep the crowd because the crowd is not His goal. He willfully and intentionally speaks hard things to the crowd to take some from the fan club to the inner circle.

The tension that many of us face is that we think we are part of the inner circle. A quick google search for "how much does the average American give to charity" spits back $850. American, not Christian. Charity, not church. I don't know if that is a true number or not, but it is the type of quick search we could do when we file our taxes. We give our accountant our giving record of $1,000 from the previous year. Having just googled and seen $850, we feel really good about our $1,000 because it is more than the average American. We feel committed to our finances. But are we? Does Jesus see it that way? Would He look at how much we spend on the cell phone and think, "yup, I am sure the priority in his life?"

Commitment is a matter of priorities. Like we said, you can be committed to many things in life, much of which we would consider to be good things. However, if you are committed to many good things, you will be committed to no great things. If you try to commit to everything, you will commit to nothing. Commitment to Jesus is a matter of priority. This is why Jesus starts with using the word "hate."

We must not read our American culture into Jesus' command to hate our families. The way Jesus' audience would understand this command is not to hate like you and I see it. The way Jesus speaks throughout the Bible makes that clear. We are told to honor our families, take care of and provide for our families. So, something else must be meant here. In that culture, this was a matter of priority. This word is used in Genesis 25 of Esau who hated his birthright, having chosen a bowl of soup instead of the blessing that was rightfully his. It was misguided priority. In Genesis 29, Abraham is said to have love for Rachel and hatred for Leah. As the story played out, it is not hatred as we tend to describe hatred. It is not hostility. The narrative shows Rachel was favored and of greater priority.

This is what Jesus is speaking of when He uses the word hate. He wants to be *the* top priority. He is not asking disciples to treat people with hostility. Remember in Luke 9 when the disciples asked Jesus if He wanted them to call fire down from Heaven to destroy some people. Yup, that was a good one. Jesus did not give in to their hate. They were wrong and misguided. No fire came down from Heaven that day! Have you made a decisive decision to make God number one in your life, to the point where all other relationships are a distant second? To the point they may think you hate them because your love for God is such a priority? Does this include the priority of self? **True followers prioritize their relationship with Jesus.**

Jesus goes on to speak of the cross. Now at this point, Jesus has not taken up the cross Himself. There has been no Good Friday and Easter Sunday yet. If I am walking in the disciples' sandals, this is confusing. This is easier for you and me to understand because we have history on our side. We know the cross in the backdrop of resurrection, at this point they did not. Jesus is calling them, void of this reference point, to be willing to die a criminal's death. He is calling them to follow Him to the cross. It is a true commitment to their lives. It is a willingness to lay down our lives in the ugliest and most humiliating manner.

And we think our commitment is "enough?" I will dig deeper into this next chapter, however, it must be mentioned now. Jesus said there is no greater love than to lay down your life for your friends (John 15:13). To commit one's life at this level is the greatest form of commitment. To my living brothers and sisters, stop complaining about your commitment. Our complaints insult our brothers and sisters in their graves who sacrificed it all. Most importantly, our complaints insult the One who gave it all. I have cleaned the church 30 Saturday's in a row. Praise God if that is the hardest thing you must do for Christ in your lifetime. Is your life, day in and day out, at the disposal of the King? **True followers bear their cross.**

Jesus goes on to talk about situations which require a little bit of planning. To make a tower and take on a construction project requires work before you break ground. You draw up plans, pull permits, assemble crews, and collect funding. A tower is a big undertaking. Jesus is not referencing the DIY project you've got going on in your backyard. This is something of worth and significance requiring you to do your homework before you start doing the work.

Then he speaks of a ruler planning for war. One side clearly has the numbers. Why would you not take this into account? If outmatched, would you send troops to die? Or send the delegation for terms of peace? Your pre-planning determines the plan to be executed. In Jesus' words, you know the right way to move forward when you count the cost. You know the commitment needed to accomplish what needs to be completed.

Jesus is not trying to scare us away, He is making us aware. It is worth considering what commitment looks like to Christ so we don't complain when it is time to live out that commitment. When it is time to live out our commitment, we knew it was coming and expected it because we had counted the cost. We commit ourselves with knowledge. We do so because the high price of commitment is worth it in light of the One who gave it all for you and I. Jesus counted the cost and declared you and I worth it, we do likewise. **True followers count the cost.**

Jesus uses a harsh word to drive home how this will cost us. It is a powerful and extreme word. I do not think many of us know the full weight of it. Count the cost, because commitment will demand you *renounce* all else. Search "define renounce" in Google, and it will spit back "formally declare one's abandonment of, refuse or resign a right or position." Think about this. Count the cost. If Jesus is *the* top priority, if we are at the point of giving Him our lives and we have counted the cost, naturally we must renounce all. To *formally declare* means we announce our renouncement. It is a stake in the ground, and our line in the sand. It is saying to all, "you are not a top priority in my life." It is looking at all those things that used to hold the top spot and saying, "you are no longer the top dog." Does your wife know she is second only to Christ? Have you married a woman who is good with that? This is renouncing aspects of the old life that were our "right and position" and saying I fill those spots with Christ. It is giving what was in our power and putting them in the mighty hands of Christ. It is taking our free will and bowing to His will.

Do all those good things no longer matter? No! Even Jesus valued His mom from the cross when He asked John to take care of her. Renouncing here means putting things in the proper place. It is saying all the good aspects of my life will be funneled through the most essential aspect of my life; my faith. You are renouncing the top spot you gave to the old aspects of life that never ultimately fulfilled you. **True followers renounce all.**

If we do all this, what can we anticipate? The salt life! There is a positive and a negative side to what Christ expresses here. There is a simple but hard truth here. Let me pose it in a question: do you want to be seen as a useful Christian or unuseful Christian? A genuinely committed Christian is useful to the King of Kings. The uncommitted lack usefulness to our Lord. To be blunt, if you can't commit, what use are you? The kingdom of God does not need useless disciples in the same manner a household does not need washed-out salt. Here Jesus uses salt, taken from the Dead Sea, to describe the negative side. It was washed out, deluded, and useless!

In Matthew 5, Jesus uses salt to say something similar: "You are the salt of the earth, but if salt has lost its taste, how shall its saltiness be restored? It is no longer good for anything except to be thrown out and trampled under people's feet." (Matthew 5:13). Similar yes, but here He states the positive side. We are to be salt. We are to be tasty. We are to embody a preservative nature, helping others stay fresh. We are to awaken flavor. When people spend time with us, read our social, or communicate with us, what does Jesus taste like to them? What flavor of our King do we leave them with? Are we committed to salting the world around us for the glory of God? **True followers of Jesus taste good!**

Ok, we see Christ's high call for His disciples to be committed to Him. Jesus, as the Son of God, is expressing the heart of God. So here are seven marks of someone successful as a committed Christian. Is it an exhaustive list? No. Is it a start? Yes.

7 Marks of Someone Successful
in the Area of Commitment

Committed Beyond Feelings

Feelings. Feelings drive us. They can drive us up as much as they can drive us down. Feelings are the lens most of us view life. Feelings help us see the world positively. Feelings help us see the world negatively. We do not do much in life because "I don't feel like it." We do many things in life despite our feelings. Which is it for the Christian? Committed Christians know how to have feelings while learning how to submit feelings to the will of God. Feelings are not bad. God created us as feelers. The question is, will we remain committed, bringing God worship in our feelings?

Jeremiah, as he lamented declared **"But this I call to mind, and therefore I have hope: The steadfast love of the Lord never ceases; his mercies never come to an end; they are new every morning; great is your faithfulness."** (Lamentation 3:21-23)

When he lost everything and his wife tested his commitment by telling him to curse God and die, Job responded, **"You speak as one of the foolish women would speak. Shall we receive good from God, and shall we not receive evil?" In all this Job did not sin with his lips."** (Job 2:10)

Joseph lived a life of ups and downs, from jail to power: a slave, a prisoner, forgotten, and all because he was sold out by his own brothers. He stayed committed to his God through the hardship, declaring to his brothers in the end: **"As for you, you meant evil against me, but God meant it for good, to bring it about that many people should be kept alive, as they are today."** (Genesis 50:20)

Perhaps the poster child of feelings, David, wrote much poetry. He sat hiding in caves and ruled from the throne. He ran after Goliath and learned to run from enemies. In Psalm 13 he starts with an expression of his feelings, saying: **"How long, O Lord? Will you forget me forever? How long will you hide your face from me?** (Psalm 13:1). Great, but how does he end the Psalm? Back to the truth. **"But I have trusted in your steadfast love; my**

heart shall rejoice in your salvation. I will sing to the Lord because he has dealt bountifully with me." (Psalm 13:5-6)

Committed to trusting God beyond his feelings, Abraham trusted God when asked to sacrifice his son: Proving trust and a willingness while praising God, he did not have to go through with it. He expressed to his son, **"Abraham said, "God will provide for himself the lamb for a burnt offering, my son."** (Genesis 22:8)

Most of these situations did not make sense. All of these situations conjure up feelings. I mean you read them and you have feelings about them. So, if we have feelings reading them, imagine living them! But these are just a few examples of faithful Christians staying committed despite their feelings. As slaves to Christ, our feelings must bow before our Master.

Remember the parable we mentioned in Chapter 1? Let's revisit it for a second,

> **7 "Will any one of you who has a servant plowing or keeping sheep say to him when he has come in from the field, 'Come at once and recline at table'? 8 Will he not rather say to him, 'Prepare supper for me, and dress properly, and serve me while I eat and drink, and afterward you will eat and drink'? 9 Does he thank the servant because he did what was commanded? 10 So you also, when you have done all that you were commanded, say, 'We are unworthy servants; we have only done what was our duty.'"** Luke 17:7-10

Here Jesus makes it clear, we must serve our Master even when we do not feel like it. At the end of the day, we have a duty to do what we may not feel like doing: will we remain committed to what is before us? In light of our Master, will we elevate His worth beyond what we feel like doing? Will we stay committed when we feel tired? Will we stay committed when we feel like focusing on another? Will we stay committed when we feel our will is better than His will? Will we remain committed, reminding the lies within our feelings of the truth we know to be true?

Sitting in Starbucks as I write this chapter, I am just a few tables over from a powerful conversation I had yesterday. I spoke with a young lady whom we can call Mildred. I don't know why but "Mildred" is always my go-to secret name, ha! Anyway, my executive pastor and I met with the only 27-year-old named Mildred. She is someone who, two months ago, lost her dad. A few months before that she lost her grandma. Her best friend is getting married and although she naturally understands why their friendship has changed, she still feels the change. She has feelings of hurt and loneliness with her current church and is finding it to be a challenging place to heal. On top of that, she has a burden for missions in Africa. The training would impact her current housing, as her current housing is linked to her job. Leaving the job would necessitate finding a place to live. She struggles with people-pleasing, saying no, and taking a Sabbath. She is drowning.

Yet can I tell you something? I'm describing her current situation with my own implied feelings. I don't know if it was the remarkably large iced coffee from the Starbucks secret menu or her faith in Christ, but she described life with incredible confidence. And P.S. I know it is her faith in Jesus. How many young women her age, with natural anxiety struggles, would be running from Jesus? Her faith has her more committed than ever as Jesus walks with her through the struggles. With commitment and resolve on full display, Mildred is the healthiest I have ever seen her as she works WITH God through the hardships.

Committed in Public and Private

An integer is a whole and complete number. No fraction and no decimal. Same root as **integrity**. Integrity describes a life that is whole and complete. Life isn't fractured. Life is complete. A whole life is the same day in and day out, weekends, nights, etc. Integrity is a life that is the same in public and private. If you are a pastor, worship leader or in public ministry, the life you project from the stage and on social media is the same as life behind the scenes. If you are a parent, if it is not ok for your kids, it's not ok for you. You would never declare, "do as I say, not as I do," but do you live like that? The same integrity demanded at your job, you demand of yourself at home. Would the people at the bar be shocked to find you on stage at a church the following day?

Proverbs has much to say on the subject of integrity;

Whoever walks in integrity walks securely, but he who makes his ways crooked will be found out. Proverbs 10:9

The integrity of the upright guides them, but the crookedness of the treacherous destroys them. Proverbs 11:3

Better is a poor person who walks in his integrity than one who is crooked in speech and is a fool. Proverbs 19:1

The righteous who walks in his integrity— blessed are his children after him! Proverbs 20:7

Better is a poor man who walks in his integrity than a rich man who is crooked in his ways. Proverbs 28:6

There is much to learn from these verses. Those with integrity are secure. Integrity is a way of life that guides us through life. Gaining less with integrity is better than gaining without integrity. Integrity is synonymous with righteousness. The poor with integrity in this world are better than those who seem to have the world but lack integrity.

Those that lack integrity have much to lose. They will be found out. They are not secure. Destruction looms for them. With that, their life is a house of cards. They will experience gains in this life, but their gains will not matter in the life to come.

At the moment, I want riches. At the moment, I want fame. At the moment, I want a following. At the moment, I want the success described in Proverbs had by those who lack integrity. Do you catch that? The way Proverbs describes those who lack integrity are the people we would see as successful. So as the committed walk with Jesus publicly, privately, on social media, when they are with people, and when they are alone, such integrity often will not come with significant earthly gains. Embrace it. Do not let a lack of worldly success pressure you to lack integrity. Perhaps that lack of earthly success is what God sees as successful because He sees your commitment to integrity.

Committed in Prayer

The most committed Christians I know have a powerful prayer life. This one aspect might be the most overlooked characteristic of a committed Christian.

As a pastor, I have many conversations with people about faith. Here are two things I hear, sadly too often in the same conversation: "I don't read my Bible, but I pray all the time. I pray every day." Moments later, after being asked about prayer, "Prayer is confusing, I don't really understand how to pray." I mean, you're already thinking it, right? Makes no sense. But, honestly, versions of these comments are something I encounter often- a declaration of a prayer life followed by confusion around prayer.

How can a committed Christian not be committed to prayer? Remember how S.D. Gordan said prayer is a necessity for those on the front lines? In essence, it is how we, Christ's warriors, get to call home base asking for reinforcements. A Christian who doesn't feel the necessity of prayer is a Christian with some gaping issues with commitment. Are you not committed to Christ in a manner that will stretch you? Are you not committed to a God-sized vision where you need God to show up and show off? Do you not interact with lost people with a heart that desperately wants them to know the love of the Father? How are we not praying for these individuals?

In my world, as a pastor of a church, you would assume this goes without saying. It should be a safe assumption, but it is not. I read the book "How to Break Church Growth Barriers" by Warren Bird. It's a book that was made for me as a competitive guy. Remember the intro and chapter one? I have since donated the book because it is irrelevant in our COVID world. However, my takeaway from the book is still in play. You must have a growing prayer life if you want a growing church. You must be dedicated to praying as if it all depends on God. Does this mean you will have growth? Nope. No is still an answer to prayer. Gideon was successful not with a larger army but with a smaller one. The point Bird made, as I remember it, was that successful pastors of growing and healthy congregations shared a characteristic of a vibrant prayer life. My prayer habits changed after I read that book.

Who is the most successful person ever to walk the earth? Do not spend too much time thinking; state the obvious- JESUS! The majority of the gospels spend time on Christ's public ministry, a ministry of about 3 years! Jesus accomplished much in a short amount of time. Here are a few verses about His commitment to prayer;

And rising very early in the morning, while it was still dark, he departed and went out to a desolate place, and there he prayed. Mark 1:35

16 But he would withdraw to desolate places and pray. Luke 5:16

And after he had dismissed the crowds, he went up on the mountain by himself to pray. When evening came, he was there alone Matthew 14:23

In these days he went out to the mountain to pray, and all night he continued in prayer to God. Luke 6:12

God is calling us into a ministry that depends on Him. Are we praying like it? What is before us only has eternal worth if it is all about Jesus. With a focus on Jesus, shouldn't we be committed to praying just like our Jesus? If our endeavor can be accomplished in our strength and efforts, there is a sense that we are 'god.' We are in control. It is within our power and ability to achieve. Man, I want something bigger. I want something that forces a struggle. I don't want easy. I can handle easy. I want to accomplish the not-so-easy. This type of life, a life that will bring struggle, will require me to depend on the Holy Spirit. Such dependence MUST drive us to our knees in prayer. It's hard to "pray without ceasing" (1 Thessalonians 5:17) if one is not committed to prayer.

Committed to progress

When I preach, I try to create tension in the opening moments of my sermon. I try to develop a sense of conflict. I then spend the remaining portion of my time addressing that conflict. This past week, I preached a sermon on this very topic. The conflict? This side of Heaven we will never be an entirely successful Christian; we will always experience failure. Welp, it's been real, we had a good run. No one here on earth will reach a state of perfection. Perfection comes in glory. Plenty of people walk around acting as if they are perfect, but it is just that, an act. For the rest of us humans who are not acting, we must be committed to progress. The goal is perfection, but measured by progress. We are like a gymnast doing a floor routine or a figure skater doing their routine. The second there is a mistake the chances for a perfect 10 goes out the window. Since sin is true of every one of us, a perfect 10 can't be accomplished by any of us. So with the goal of perfection still before us, what are we committed to? Progress.

John 21 is one of my favorite passages in all the Scriptures because I can see myself as I read the narrative. Jesus has been arrested, betrayed, denied, abandoned, killed, and is now resurrected. Some of His best friends are out fishing, and Jesus walks up to the shore. They do not realize it is Him until there is a massive catch of fish. 153 to be exact. Peter, realizing it is Jesus, jumps ship! And here we ask, what is it about Peter that this dude can't stay IN A BOAT?! Swimming to shore, he meets Jesus cooking some fish over a charcoal fire. Peter was warming himself with the same type of fire when he denied Jesus. Think the smell of a charcoal fire brought him back to the biggest failure he had ever experienced? Certainly. The conversation that follows rocks me;

> **15 When they had finished breakfast, Jesus said to Simon Peter, "Simon, son of John, do you love me more than these?" He said to him, "Yes, Lord; you know that I love you." He said to him, "Feed my lambs." 16 He said to him a second time, "Simon, son of John, do you love me?" He said to him, "Yes, Lord; you know that I love you." He said to him, "Tend my sheep." 17 He said to him the third time, "Simon, son of John, do you love me?" Peter was grieved because he said to him the third time, "Do you love me?" and he said to him, "Lord, you know everything; you know that I love you." Jesus said to him, "Feed my sheep. 18 Truly, truly, I say to you, when you were young, you used to dress yourself and walk wherever you wanted, but when you are old, you will stretch out your hands, and another will dress you and carry you where you do not want to go." John 21:15-18**

There is so much here, especially when you dig into the Greek. For our purpose, here is what I want us to see. True love drives us FORWARD. Jesus is not reprimanding Peter, Peter has already emotionally beaten himself up. Feeling like a failure, he was back into the fishing business. Jesus did not see his failure as ministry ending, rather, as only Christ can do, it was ministry propelling. Peter, who tried doing life with his own strength, was humbled.

Now he moves forward, not in his strength but in the strength of Jesus. Here Jesus is not saying you are washed up. He is looking at Peter and saying, do you love me? Ya? THEN WE HAVE WORK TO DO! What are you doing with this fishing business? I want you to be fishers of men! You love me, Peter? It's time to move on and move forward. Peter may have fished again, but it is never recorded in Scripture. This new re-committed Peter would be used by God to lead 3,000 men to come to know Jesus as Lord and Savior. 3,000 people roughly two months after denying the Lord Jesus. We must be committed to progress. Grow out of failure. Learn from failure. Seek not to repeat the same failures. Do a sober-self assessment with this one focus; am I progressing? Am I growing? Commit yourself to progress.

Committed to His Mission

The Pharisees had the appearance of commitment, yet with hearts far from God. They did not chase after what God chased after. They were committed to religion. So, were they committed? Yes. Was God pleased with their commitment? No. How many Christians have not shared the gospel with a single person in the last year? Five years? A lifetime? How can a church have no baptisms year after year? HOW CAN THAT BE? It displays a misguided commitment. We live in a world that wants to be *instafamous*, so why risk what could lead people to think of us differently? The committed Christian cares MOST about what the Lord of Lords thinks of his or her life. What does the Lord of Lords think of how you are doing with the mission He has left for you?

Upon leaving this earth, Jesus said this in Matthew 28, a passage we have come to call the "Great Commission:"

> **And Jesus came and said to them, "All authority in heaven and on earth has been given to me. 19 Go therefore and make disciples of all nations, baptizing them in the name of the Father and of the Son and of the Holy Spirit, 20 teaching them to observe all that I have commanded you. And behold, I am with you always, to the end of the age."** Matthew 28:18-20

This Great Commission has become our *Great Omission*. Jesus has all authority. His authority gives Him the ability to direct. If He has all authority, we have no room to assume authority. So if Christ, with all authority, has given us marching orders, this is what we ought to be committed to. We are told to go. We are told to make disciples. We are told to baptize people. We are told to guide people to observe what Christ has commanded. And we are told we will not do this alone, that Christ will be with us through it. Want to feel the presence of God? Start pursuing the mission of God! Are there people stronger in their faith because of your involvement in their lives? Are there people living more holy lives because of your involvement? Not holy as the Pharisees appeared holy, holy like Christ! Has anyone been baptized in the last few years because of your involvement in their lives? Is there a "going" aspect to our commitment? When we cross the finish line and see Jesus face to face, what will He think of our commitment to Him if we were never used by Him to lead a single person across the threshold of faith?

In Luke 14, Jesus has an interesting dinner party with some Pharisees. He describes His heart and whom He wishes to be at His table. He then goes on to describe what being all in looks like. We examined the last portion of that section earlier in this chapter. So directly after rebuking the Pharisees for exclusion and declaring plainly the all-in nature of commitment, Luke records this;

> **Now the tax collectors and sinners were all drawing near to hear him.2 And the Pharisees and the scribes grumbled, saying, "This man receives sinners and eats with them." 3 So he told them this parable: 4 "What man of you, having a hundred sheep, if he has lost one of them, does not leave the ninety-nine in the open country, and go after the one that is lost, until he finds it? 5 And when he has found it, he lays it on his shoulders, rejoicing. 6 And when he comes home, he calls together his friends and his neighbors, saying to them, 'Rejoice with me, for I have found my sheep that was lost.' 7 Just so, I tell you, there will be more joy in heaven over one sinner who repents than over ninety-nine righteous persons who need no repentance.** Luke 15:1-7

Literally books have been written about this passage. We will not deep dive it here, although trust me, I want to. For our purpose, look at how Jesus redirects the Pharisees. Look at how He challenges their commitment. Are they committed to seeking and saving the lost? Are they committed to finding the sick, getting them to the hospital, and making them better? Are they committed to the search and rescue party? They love their holy rollers' party, while Christ throws a party for the pimp who turns to Him in faith. Pray for One. Seek the One. Commit to finding the One.

Committed to Producing Fruit

Being surrounded by the unholy has a way of developing the most unholy of lives. Those complacent in faith and lacking commitment will seek the one but not for the sake of the mission. They want to be relevant. They want to be relatable. You cannot live like the lost hoping to reach the lost. Why? You are one of them and need to "be reached." If you are committed to the ways of God, your life will produce different fruit than the unsaved. Christ Himself used the analogy of fruit;

> **15 "Beware of false prophets, who come to you in sheep's clothing but inwardly are ravenous wolves. 16 You will recognize them by their fruits. Are grapes gathered from thornbushes or figs from thistles? 17 So, every healthy tree bears good fruit, but the diseased tree bears bad fruit. 18 A healthy tree cannot bear bad fruit, nor can a diseased tree bear good fruit.19 Every tree that does not bear good fruit is cut down and thrown into the fire. 20 Thus you will recognize them by their fruits.** Matthew 7:15-20

How do we know who is committed to Christ and who is not? - by their fruit. Honestly, this is obvious. But I must admit, I forgot about this aspect when mapping out this book. In each section where we describe the distinguishing marks of a successful person in a given area, I poll social media and text a handful of people whose opinions I value. This was the most common response back to the question, "what characteristics do you expect to find from those considered a 'committed Christian?'" Over and over again, I got the "fruit of the Spirit." Think about that, this right here is what a multitude of mature Christians point to as a sign of commitment. You have Christians taking Christ's words seriously! Want to know if a Christian is truly committed? Examine the fruit! Examine the right metrics. The fruit the world produces or expects to see is not the fruit Christ is concerned with. As we have said throughout this book, God and the world work on different metric systems. The fruit the world is looking for is more relationships, money, power, stuff, homes, et cetera. Christ wants more as well. But the more that Christ expects is different from the more the world expects. Christ wants more of:

> **But the fruit of the Spirit is love, joy, peace, patience, kindness, goodness, faithfulness, 23 gentleness, self-control; against such things, there is no law.** Galatians 5:22-23

The second you say yes to a relationship with Jesus Christ, the Holy Spirit lives inside you. When Jesus is embraced, the Holy Spirit gets placed! The Holy Spirit gets to work producing this fruit in your life. The first litmus test is to examine your life and say, "is there more of this fruit in my life?" Grab a journal and take eight days to do a sober-self assessment of your life. On day one write "love" at the top of the page. Start journaling about how Christ defines love, then journal about the old you regarding love. After that, consider yourself in the present: Are you more or less loving? And finally, answer this question: If I were to let the Holy Spirit develop me into a more loving person, what would change about me? There are your marching orders moving forward. Do that for eight straight days replacing "love" with a new fruit of the Spirit. This has shown me I have grown, but Jason, we have some work to do!

You have a daily decision to make: Will I die to myself and allow the Holy Spirit to do the work He is supposed to do in my life? You, as a Christian, still have free will. You are free to make choices. Your choices display your commitment. Are you committed to the process the Holy Spirit is looking to do in your life? Specifically, the process of being made into the likeness of Jesus Christ! Before you start making excuses, following Jesus will cost you your 'but.' "I don't have time to be in God's Word." But you have time for hours on social media. "I don't have time to journal and consider the fruit of the Spirit." But you have time to watch hours of sports. This is a process. Do you really want to tell God you cannot commit to the process when He knows how you spend every minute of the day? The time you invest produces fruit. Invest into the things of God and produce the things of God. Invest into sports, Xbox, and social media and produce what is currently being produced.

Perhaps social anxiety is growing because of our growing investment in social media.

Committed here with a hunger for more

This is a "both/ and" type of commitment. For me, if this commitment is out of balance, I will soon find myself out of balance. This commitment says, "I am committed and content with what is before me, while desiring more." I am committed to my church in two locations. It's been a move of God to get us to this place. Yet, I pray for the day we are in five locations. I am committed to Todd, my neighbor who has said yes to a relationship with Jesus, is now a partner in our church, and will soon lead his own life group. Yet, I am praying for more. Bo Chancey, the Lead Pastor of One Church in New Hampshire, often says; "as many people as quickly as possible in the Kingdom of God." The Christian is not committed to conquering and moving on. We see that in the Great Commission we examined earlier. We are to make more and more disciples, yet discipleship is a process.

Paul was a great example of this all-in commitment. In Acts 14, we see a very clear example of this concept:

> **19 But Jews came from Antioch and Iconium, and having persuaded the crowds, they stoned Paul and dragged him out of the city, supposing that he was dead. 20 But when the disciples gathered about him, he rose up and entered the city, and on the next day he went on with Barnabas to Derbe.21 When they had preached the gospel to that city and had made many disciples, they returned to Lystra and to Iconium and to Antioch, 22 strengthening the souls of the disciples, encouraging them to continue in the faith, and saying that through many tribulations we must enter the kingdom of God.23 And when they had appointed elders for them in every church, with prayer and fasting they committed them to the Lord in whom they had believed.** Acts 14:19-23

We have read this passage showing Paul's grit to be left for dead and go back into the city among the people who had tried to kill him. The dude's crazy y'all. It takes a particular type of person to get yo' butt beat and then get back up to go back in. Paul was committed to seeing more people come to know Jesus as Lord and Savior. Perhaps it was the sight of genuine commitment that helped people see the genuineness of the message. More people came to know Jesus because of this type of commitment. Paul wanted more and more people. However, this was not his only focus.

The passage also shows Paul traveling back to his sending church in Antioch, hitting Lystra and Iconium along the way. These are churches he helped to establish. These churches were out of the way. There were shorter routes back to Antioch. Paul just got his butt beat. For you and I, wouldn't we rationalize the need for a break? A vacation? I think Paul had earned a vacation, no? But instead of rushing back to his people in Antioch for some needed R & R, he hit up Lystra and Iconium. Why? To establish leadership there and develop a system that would reach more people while protecting the church's health.

We must commit to strengthening our current good habits while learning new habits. We must commit to reaching more people for Christ while helping others grow in their walk with Christ. We must attend the small group and the outreach. We must read our Bible in the morning and eat with sinners in the evening. We must be wise with the money we have while praying for more to be generous with. We learn to be faithful with the little before us, hoping to be trusted with more to come.

Maintaining priorities in the present while keeping your eyes on the horizon will require you to master the word "NO." Those with great hunger often fall prey to every good thing that comes their way. Those that keep chasing GOOD never accomplish anything GREAT. Jesus exemplified this ability.

The Example of Jesus

Commitment is a matter of choice. You have the power and ability to do anything, but you choose to commit to what is before you. Perhaps the most powerful people are those with the willpower to say no. Steve Jobs excelled at this, he once said;

"People think focus means saying yes to the thing you've got to focus on. But that's not what it means at all. It means saying no to the hundred other good ideas that there are. You have to pick carefully. I'm actually as proud of the things we haven't done as the things I have done. Innovation is saying no to 1,000 things."

Was Jesus a committed person? He committed Himself to dying. He was obedient unto death (Phil. 2:8). He had the willpower to say no and the ability to withhold in order to set himself up for the best yes. In the garden, while praying, he committed to drink the cup if the Father would not take it from Him. He then had a moment to remind the disciples of what He could do but would choose not to do;

> **50 Jesus said to him, "Friend, do what you came to do." Then they came up and laid hands on Jesus and seized him. 51 And behold, one of those who were with Jesus stretched out his hand and drew his sword and struck the servant of the high priest and cut off his ear. 52 Then Jesus said to him, "Put your sword back into its place. For all who take the sword will perish by the sword. 53 Do you think that I cannot appeal to my Father, and he will at once send me more than twelve legions of angels?** Matthew 26:50-53

There is growing tension, things are getting bad and will only get worse. A dude just lost his ear. Peter, whom we know was the swordsman, apparently was not gifted with the sword. Unless he intended to cut the guy's ear off, then he is impressive. When we get to heaven, let's all challenge Peter to a dual. Fun. Anyway, the duel is ok. Jesus is there to heal a guy present to harm Him. Do you catch at the end what is within His ability? To utter perhaps a single word, "come." To look to heaven and scream, "SEND THEM." And then legions and legions of angels would be present to fight, defend, and destroy. Could you imagine the scene in heaven? We think about Christ's death from our retrospective perspective, but what about heaven, as the angels and the Father are stare down watching the scene unfold? Was the Father crying? Enraged? Were the angels chomping at the bit waiting for the command to come down to defend? Jesus never lost His cool and never uttered the command that could end all the pain. He was committed to get Himself to the cross. He was committed to obedience. This commitment required Him to deny what was in His ability to do.

Christ's commitment immediately impacted criminals: Barabbas and some thieves. Barabbas was released for crimes deserving of death, all because he happened to be in jail at just the right time. Christ's commitment to get Himself to the cross had a direct impact on Barabbas, who was released from jail. A man deserving of punishment found freedom because of Christ's commitment. Sound familiar? Hope so. It is the same freedom offered to you and me from the jail of our sin—more on that in Chapter 7.

He is committed to get Himself to the cross. He is standing trial. Says very little. He does not try to defend Himself. He is committed to getting Himself to that cross. When His body is literally broken, another guy named Simon steps in and carries the cross on the final leg of the journey. Jesus is committed to get Himself to that cross.

Did He call the angels when the soldiers mocked Him? Punched Him? Shoved nail-like thorns into His skull? No. Did He call the angels when he was punched and spit on by religious leaders? No. Did He call the angels as the whip ripped open His back? No. Did He call the angels with each hammer stroke as the nails fell deeper and deeper into His flesh? No. Why? He was committed to run His race and finish what had been set before Him.

And there, on that hill we call calvary, Jesus never called for the calvary. One thief mocked Him, the other worshiped Him. One thief hanging next to Jesus on his own cross did not receive the temporary freedom that Barabbas received. This one thief found true freedom in Christ, he committed himself to the Savior hanging next to him.

39 One of the criminals who were hanged railed at him, saying, "Are you not the Christ? Save yourself and us!" 40 But the other

rebuked him, saying, "Do you not fear God, since you are under the same sentence of condemnation? 41 And we indeed justly, for we are receiving the due reward of our deeds; but this man has done nothing wrong." 42 And he said, "Jesus, remember me when you come into your kingdom."43 And he said to him, "Truly, I say to you, today you will be with me in paradise." Luke 23:39-43

Jesus was committed to being obedient to the very end, scorning the shame of the cross (Heb. 12:2), and completing the mission to be the sacrificial lamb for all humanity. And in the end, He showed great commitment to the bigger picture while caring for the individual before Him. Jesus did not see the thief next to Him as a waste of breath. He did not say, "I've got my own things to worry about as I hang here." He did not disregard the individual because of the greater purpose behind the moment. With some of Jesus' final words, one more person became a citizen of heaven. Leading up to this moment, there were a whole lot of unsaid yeses and timely no's making it possible. There is a thief in heaven because Jesus held the angels back.

What is Biblical success? *Biblical success is when God's heart and God's ways become my heart and my way.* Want to be successful in the eyes of God? Be a person characterized by exceedingly great commitment.

INGREDIENT #3: COMMITMENT
BIBLICAL CASE STUDY

"Let not steadfast love and faithfulness forsake you; bind them around your neck" (Proverbs 3:3)

"Integrity is keeping a commitment even after circumstances have changed." **David Jeremiah**

Biblical success is when God's ways and God's heart become my way and my heart. Are we, those dearly loved by God, committed to a life pursuing a mantra like this? As stated previously, Elizabeth Elliot once said, "To pray, 'thy will be done' I must be willing, if that answer requires it, that my will be undone." You and I wake up each morning with the same battle, it is a battle of wills. Whose will is going to win the day? Yours or God's? To allow God's heart and God's ways to become my ways and my heart will require you to be perpetually undone. As God's will is carried out in your life, your commitment will be displayed in your integrity.

Golf is a game of integrity and etiquette. However, my version of golf is a little different. I enjoy golf. I shoot in the 90's to low 100's. I'm an average weekend golfer. If you are unfamiliar with golf, the world's best would likely shoot the ball about 45 times less than I do. At my level of golf, we break certain rules and some of the etiquette. We fart and burp to break the silence while someone is swinging. We may even cut a hole in our pockets. Why? So, when we hit a ball out of bounds, you can drop a new ball through your pocket and out your pant leg. Then you say, "I found my ball which happens to be in bounds!" We get mulligans. You just expect it at my level of golf. At the highest level? I would be considered a cheat displaying a colossal lack of integrity, showing no commitment to the rules.

I am the exact opposite of Bobby Jones. He won nine major championships. He had a Hall of Fame golf game. Do you know what else he had? Hall of Fame integrity. During one tournament, Jones assessed himself a one-stroke penalty for addressing a ball while it was ever so slightly moving. No one, media, fan, or competitor, saw it. The only one that knew Jones unknowingly committed a penalty was Jones. He was committed to do what was right. When no one else knew, Jones still assessed himself a one-stroke penalty. By how many strokes did Jones lose the tournament? One. At the end of the tournament, reporters praised him for his exceptional integrity. Jones is said to have fired back, "You might as well praise a man for not robbing a bank as to praise him for playing by the rules." "Do I assess myself a one-stroke penalty?" This is only a question for those who lack commitment to the rules. It is not a dilemma for a person of integrity.

We also do not feel the dilemma within our commitment when we think of ourselves better than we are. We believe our commitment is high and our integrity is spotless. In reality, it is lacking. We are great at having an overinflated view of ourselves. Why? We live in a world of comparison. We scroll and troll through social media where we see news stories of awful people. Or, like my buddy we mentioned a few chapters ago, we set the bar at the average gang member. When we compare ourselves to the world, we will always walk away with an overinflated view of our commitment and integrity. Is the world the bar? Has it ever been the bar?

Christ is the bar. We do not strive to be slightly above average, we strive to be like Christ. This is why a life of total integrity and full commitment to Christ is increasingly rare. The moral bar of society is shifting lower. If society is the bar, then the moral standards within the church also shift lower. After all, if we are satisfied with being slightly above average, that bar will shift as society shifts. Here we are content giving God our last fruits instead of our first fruit. The last fruits in a world with no fruit is slightly above average.

In this chapter, we will walk in the sandals of three young men residing in a land as exiles. They were not born there. These Israelites have been taken from Israel and exiled to Babylon. We will look at how they handled immense pressure to lower the standard of their faith. We will see how they lived a life of resolve. As we learn to walk in their sandals, we will learn to increase our commitment to the cause of Christ.

Here is the situation these three Jewish boys find themselves in:

> **King Nebuchadnezzar made an image of gold, whose height was sixty cubits and its breadth six cubits. He set it up on the plain of Dura, in the province of Babylon. 2 Then King Nebuchadnezzar sent to gather the satraps, the prefects, and the governors, the counselors, the treasurers, the justices, the magistrates, and all the officials of the provinces to come to the dedication of the image that King Nebuchadnezzar had set up. 3 Then the satraps, the prefects, and the governors, the counselors, the treasurers, the justices, the magistrates, and all the officials of the provinces gathered for the dedication of the image that King Nebuchadnezzar had set up. And they stood before the image that Nebuchadnezzar had set up. 4 And the herald proclaimed aloud, "You are commanded, O peoples, nations, and languages, 5 that when you hear the sound of the horn, pipe, lyre, trigon, harp, bagpipe, and every kind of music, you are to fall down and worship the golden image that King Nebuchadnezzar has set up. 6 And whoever does not fall down and worship shall immediately be cast into a burning fiery furnace." Daniel 3:1-6**

And then it plays out just like that. The music plays and mostly all bow before the statue. The who's who of the land are gathered together. These are the officials, the dignitaries, and those with responsibilities granted by the king. If you were a young Jewish man living in this foreign land, would you not feel pressure?

Pressure. The size of it creates pressure, it is 90 ft tall and 9 ft wide. Being among the who's who from all over the land creates pressure. There is a specific moment when you will have to bow or remain standing. Pressure. The warning of death would create pressure. The likelihood that you would stand alone would create pressure. Pressure fills this scene.

The current scene of your life has its pressures. As you read this, is COVID still a thing creating pressure? Is your job demanding and creating pressure? Do your finances produce pressure in your life? Is your physical health a source of pressure? Friendship? Marriage? Kids? Politics? School? We live in a day and age where we feel more pressure than any other time. I do not know the statistics but I can tell you about my current reality as a pastor in Ocean County, New Jersey. I talk to more people feeling anxiety derived from pressure and needing professional help than at any other time in my pastorate. Yet, there is no professional help available. Every single counselor I know has a waiting list. Every. Single. One. Professionals in this field are overwhelmed by the demands. So if Ocean County, New Jersey, is any indication, we all feel heightened pressure.

During the pandemic I met with Pat Engroff, an elder at my church. As an elder and friend, I knew he was on the "struggle bus." Pat's wife deals with medical issues that are not debilitating but need to be consistently managed. He has three kids bringing their own stresses and pressures to life. Pat was less than a year into owning his own plumbing business. It was growing, but not to the point where he could take a paycheck. He was working insane hours, yet financially not drawing from the business. We met COVID -style in my backyard around a campfire and through that conversation he determined he needed to sell the business. The pressure was getting to him and now legitimately impacted his physical health. So, he sold and took a more 9-5 job to invest in his family and church family.

As I write this, Pat is now an example of staying committed through pressure. The pressure he faces in life is still there. He is still a Dad. He is still walking alongside his wife through the medical aspects she is facing. He is coaching a basketball team and admits he knows nothing about basketball. But guess what? They have won two games in a row! WINNING STREAK! The point? Pat still faces pressure in everyday life. But he has learned what is an allowable amount of pressure that still has him committed to the cause of Christ. A few weekends ago, Pat helped clean the church on a Friday. He met me for breakfast on a Saturday because we hold each other accountable. Then on Sunday, he was at church at 7AM with his 12-year-old son to serve. Pat set up our parking signs and his son ran slides on our Production Team. He still has pressure, but he is committed to the cause of Christ through the pressure.

How much pressure do we feel in our faith? Does our faith create pressure? It did for the Apostle Paul. Or do we not feel the pressures of faith because we are not taking our faith seriously? Do we feel pressures in our faith because our conscience eats at us as we give our God, deserving of first fruits, our last fruits? So much in life creates pressure and places demands on our lives. Here is where pressure will reveal our modern-day idols.

Dwight Moody said, "You don't have to go to heathen lands today to find false gods. America is full of them. Whatever you love more than God is your idol." Tim Keller has also written a significant amount on this subject. He defines an idol as "anything that absorbs your heart and imagination more than God, anything you seek to give you what only God can give." For our purpose, we have to ask this question, what will we do when the pressures of idol worship come our way? Worship any statues? It still happens, but it is rare.

What about those idols in life that are inherently good? When a good thing becomes a God thing, it becomes a bad thing. It becomes an idol. Personal time is good, but has personal time become an idol? Money can be used for good, but has money become an idol? Family is good, but has family become an idol? Having a job is good, but has your job become an idol? When these good areas are elevated to unhealthy levels, 'god' level, you will begin to feel pressure. When these areas of your life create pressure, will you stand in your commitment to your faith?

12 There are certain Jews whom you have appointed over the affairs of the province of Babylon: Shadrach, Meshach, and Abednego. These men, O king, pay no attention to you; they do not serve your gods or worship the golden image that you have set up." 13 Then Nebuchadnezzar in furious rage commanded that Shadrach,

Meshach, and Abednego be brought. So they brought these men before the king. 14 Nebuchadnezzar answered and said to them, "Is it true, O Shadrach, Meshach, and Abednego, that you do not serve my gods or worship the golden image that I have set up? 15 Now if you are ready when you hear the sound of the horn, pipe, lyre, trigon, harp, bagpipe, and every kind of music, to fall down and worship the image that I have made, well and good. But if you do not worship, you shall immediately be cast into a burning fiery furnace. And who is the god who will deliver you out of my hands?" 16 Shadrach, Meshach, and Abednego answered and said to the king, "O Nebuchadnezzar, we have no need to answer you in this matter. 17 If this be so, our God whom we serve is able to deliver us from the burning fiery furnace, and he will deliver us out of your hand, O king. 18 But if not, be it known to you, O king, that we will not serve your gods or worship the golden image that you have set up." Daniel 3:12-18

"Yo king! These are your boys and they have ignored you. Yo king, they do not serve your gods." So they are brought before him. His undies are all sorts of tied in a knot. He is tripping. Yet, in his fury, he is showing mercy by giving them a second chance. "Maybe you did not hear the music." Here is a second chance to undo the situation your refusal has created. So now there is increased pressure. They are standing before the king with a second opportunity to prove their faithfulness (or from God's perspective; faithlessness). Faithful to this king or *their* King? Again it is bow or burn to test their resolve.

Whom are you resolved to honor boys? I mean, they owe King Nebuchadnezzar their livelihood. If they choose not to bow it is like they are slapping the hand that feeds them. But when slapping the hand that feeds you results in slapping the hand of God, it is no contest. Nebuchadnezzar reminds them from an earthly sense, nothing can save them from his power. "Boys, do you really want to commit to your God? Really want to go all in light of my power?"

For them? This was a non-negotiable before negotiations began. They had already signed their non-compete clause with the true King of Kings! Their commitment was not up for debate. If the challenge is to worship the one true King or the gods of this world, the decision has already been made. If it is to serve the one true God and be burned to a crisp, no contest! God wins.

Then they add this powerful "P.S.," did you catch it? "Our God can deliver if He so chooses. King Neb, know this, even if He does not, we still will not bow." They know without a shadow of a doubt that God can save them. This is the God they are loyal and committed to. They trust and know His power, yet they do not presume to know His plans. This is one of the greatest affirmations in the Bible. "Even if He does not, we will not bow!" Take that King Neb!

I was voted "most outgoing" during my senior year of high school. I knew everyone and was friends with most. I think it was my junior year of high school when I got a reputation. Oh, spicy. No, not that type of reputation. I walked into the lunch room and all the "cool kids" were at a table towards the front and to the right. Right away they called me over. So me being me, I strolled over with a good head nod and a "what up." One of the guys at the table held out a $20 and said, "curse and we will give you this $20." I was not prepared for a test I did not know was coming. I mean, here I am about to get a 50-cent slice of cardboard pizza and now I am being offered $20 for cursing.

Yes, I was a good Christian boy, but I will not pretend like the occasional curse word did not fall out of my mouth. It was not a habit for me, but sadly, it was not wholly foreign to me. However, although it was not foreign to me, this was not about if I was willing to curse. Maybe it was to them, but for me, this was a test of commitment. Would you take the cash and sin or honor God and walk? They tried making me comfortable by cursing themselves in what they were saying to entice me. For me, though, this was a non-decision. Pin me against my God, and God will always win. So I walked. My reputation? From that day on I was known as "rev."

You need to commit before a commitment is needed. It needs to be a "pre-decision" before a decision is needed. You need to be predetermined to live determined. Your mind needs to be made up before the pressure comes. What do you need to commit to now that perhaps is not a current reality?

"Lord, I commit to give you 10% if that inheritance comes my way." "Lord, if I am blessed with kids, I commit now to raise them as you would." "Lord, if my wife gets sick, I commit to love you by sticking with her through it." "Lord, last week Tom was asked to do something unethical at work. I commit to honor you even if I lose my job." "Lord, he asked his last girlfriend to come to bed with him, if he plays me like that, I promise to honor you." What do you need to commit to now? Are you predetermined to honor God when a future situation arises? These men did. Here is how it played out for them:

19 Then Nebuchadnezzar was filled with fury, and the expression of his face was changed against Shadrach, Meshach, and Abednego. He ordered the furnace heated seven times more than it was usually heated. 20 And he ordered some of the mighty men of his army to bind Shadrach, Meshach, and Abednego, and to cast them into the burning fiery furnace. 21 Then these men were bound in their cloaks, their tunics, their hats, and their other garments, and they were thrown into the burning fiery furnace. 22 Because the king's order was urgent and the furnace overheated, the flame of the fire killed those men who took up Shadrach, Meshach, and Abednego. 23 And these three men, Shadrach, Meshach, and Abednego, fell bound into the burning fiery furnace. 24 Then King Nebuchadnezzar was astonished and rose up in haste. He declared to his counselors, "Did we not cast three men bound into the fire?" They answered and said to the king, "True, O king." 25 He answered and said, "But I see four men unbound, walking in the midst of the fire, and they are not hurt; and the appearance of the fourth is like a son of the gods." 26 Then Nebuchadnezzar came near to the door of the burning fiery furnace; he declared, "Shadrach, Meshach, and Abednego, servants of the Most High God, come out, and come here!" Then Shadrach, Meshach, and Abednego came out from the fire. 27 And the satraps, the prefects, the governors, and the king's counselors gathered together and saw that the fire had not had any power over the bodies of those men. The hair of their heads was not singed, their cloaks were not harmed, and no smell of fire had come upon them. 28 Nebuchadnezzar answered and said, "Blessed be the God of

Shadrach, Meshach, and Abednego, who has sent his angel and delivered his servants, who trusted in him, and set aside the king's command, and yielded up their bodies rather than serve and worship any god except their own God. 29 Therefore I make a decree: Any people, nation, or language that speaks anything against the God of Shadrach, Meshach, and Abednego shall be torn limb from limb, and their houses laid in ruins, for there is no other god who is able to rescue in this way." 30 Then the king promoted Shadrach, Meshach, and Abednego in the province of Babylon. Daniel 3:19-30

Hear me as clearly as I can write this; God still allowed them to go into the furnace. These young men still had to walk into the furnace. God proved His faithfulness, and they proved their commitment **in the fire.** A commitment to integrity will not keep us from getting thrown into a fiery furnace, but it can keep us from getting burned. It is a statement in word and action that we would rather get in trouble with King Nebuchadnezzar than get in trouble with God. This is worship. God's pleasure was elevated over man's pleasure.

The God who was worshiped through their commitment did not deliver them from the fire but met them in the fire. In the fire, he delivered them out of the fire. What is likely a "Jesus sighting" in the Old Testament is a powerful moment. God sent His Son into the fire to meet these young men and deliver them. Jesus, the ultimate agent of deliverance! This radical deliverance is a statement to the delivered, as well as the onlookers. After calling them out and finding them completely unaffected, the king determines there is a God who can deliver! Their deliverance from the fire led to the king's reckoning with the King of Kings!

The impact on the king is seen in his decree and the promotion of the young men. The Jewish faith is not only legal, but it is also now protected. You speak against it and you will be destroyed along with your family. The men, who already hold important jobs, are promoted. What a day! Called before a statue, dragged before the king, thrown into a fiery furnace, conversation with Jesus (what must that have been like?!), faith protected, and king promoted. What a full day for these committed young men.

My church recently launched a new experience we have called "pizza church." The short of it is that we felt God calling us to reach other communities. However, our church did not have margin in kids ministry or worship ministry to multiply exactly what we are doing in Toms River (our main location). So, either ignore the calling or try something different. We like different. So we found a really nice venue and got it at an excellent rate through a connection. Through the same connection, I was introduced to someone in town who gave us a great price on pizza. And now for under $300 a week we have a new location developed around fellowship and the word. We break bread and then fill ourselves up with the word of God as I preach the same sermon from Sunday morning. It is rad.

There is a mom who has been coming from about 30 minutes away for four weeks straight. She is dragging her kids with her. Her one son does not even like pizza! She has a look on her face that I imagine these Jewish boys had, a look of determination. Life has it that the family cannot get to church on a Sunday morning, but with this commitment, she is determined to get herself and her kids to church Sunday evening. The commitment shouts her priorities. As I see her, I am reminded of my own mother.

I grew up in a cultural time where little happened on Sunday morning. It was a time when prioritizing church was not as challenging as today. Nonetheless, it was a commitment that was still tested. My mom, like this mom, was determined to get her boys to church. How old fashion, eh?! (HOW REFRESHING). When I was younger, I made all-star baseball teams. We had games on Sundays. I have literally missed all-star games to attend church. I would attend in my uniform and then we would rush to the game so I could try and catch something. If my friends slept over on a Saturday night, you just knew Jason's crazy mom was gonna drag your sorry butt out of bed and to church. If my brother and I asked to stay out late on a Saturday night, it was always a yes. Stay out late but know, Mom is gonna be up early singing "rise and shine, give God the glory glory" as she was dragging our tired butts to church. We learned to play hard and pray hard. We learned that church meant something and had great value in our lives. It taught me what commitment looks like. It taught me commitment is costly, costing you your comfort and convenience.

These three men knew this as well, commitment is costly, but God be praised. These men sold out for their God in a way our church desperately needs today. We need more men and women putting their lives into the hands of God. More men and women not bowing to comfort and convenience but bowing their lives to their Father. Men and women willing to put their lives into the hands of God. Men and women who will cease trying to take matters into their own hands. Men and women who are continually giving over to God all the dead areas of the old life. My God cannot resurrect what is not dead. Put that old dead you in the hands of God and watch that resurrection power brew out of you. Only giving God parts of yourself will have you walking around half alive because you have not fully died to self. We need more men and women with resurrection power flowing out of them because they have given all of themselves over to the King of Kings and Lord of Lords. When we do, when we make God the priority over our comfort, our convenience, and when it is costly to do so, GOD BE GLORIFIED.

If you take away anything from this commitment biblical case study, take away this; *there is nothing to solve when you live with resolve.*

There are questions and dilemmas in many of our lives that are not dilemmas or questions for people wholly committed to the cause of Christ. This was a real-life situation for these young men. This was not a question for them. When it comes time to bow, we stand. Should I read my Bible? This is not a question for the committed follower of Jesus. Should I be at church surrounded by my family? This is not a question for the committed follower of Jesus. Should I love the Lord through serving? This is not a question for the committed follower of Jesus. Should I love those around me? This is not a question for the committed follower of Jesus. Should I do all this when it is not easy, convenient or comfortable? This is not a question for the committed follower of Jesus. What cost is too much for Christ? This is not a question for the committed follower of Jesus.

To my brothers and sisters in Christ Jesus reading this, we have bowed. It is time to stand back up. It is time to give God our first fruits and not our last fruits. Yes, society gives no 'fruit' to God. I get that. I get your last fruits are better than the majority on earth. But God wants the best of your time, the best of your money, and the best of your talent. We must not "compare" this away. He deserves our best.

To my brothers in Christ Jesus reading this, where are my committed Christians? Where are my Esther's willing to say, "if I perish, I perish?" Where are my Stephens willing to declare the name of Jesus while being stoned to death? Where are my Pauls, who after being left for dead outside the city, went back in because he still had a job to do? Where are my widows, who do not have many coins to offer, but what I have, I give, God be magnified? Where are my Daniels willing to be faithful in, through, and out of the lion's den? Where are my young men, saying if I burn, I burn, I will always stand for my Jesus? Where are my Deborahs, saying to the men, "if you don't step up and fight, I, the women, will prove God's power in the fight?!" Where are my Christians saying, forget comforts, I will volunteer if there is a need? Where are my Christians saying, "I'll make the drive when leaving my house is required?" Where are my Christians saying, "if I must speak up at work, I will speak up?" Where are my Christians saying, "if anyone is going to love the person who is down and out, it will be me?" Where are my committed Christians saying, "you all can make whatever excuse you want, but for me, my anthem is 'for the One who gave it all, nothing is a sacrifice.'"

This book is prompted by a question, "your life is going to cross a finish line, all lives do. Are you content with the finish line your life is going to cross?" Midlife crisis and here we are! At that same conference, former President George W. Bush was interviewed. During his interview, he expressed the need to have clear priorities to take the decision out of decision-making. Meaning, clear priorities determine decisions before they need to be decided on. He gave this as a 'for instance' saying that one of his top priorities is valuing all human life. His pro-life stance is based on this value. You may see it as a Republican thing, but he sees it as a priority thing. To the point where, when people came to him with an initiative to send millions of dollars in foreign aid to Africa to help save lives, he said yes. Giving foreign aid seemingly on a whim is not a very Republican thing to do. But when presented with the opportunity to fight aids in Africa, his priority of human life made this an instant yes. This is when he teamed up with Bono and through the initiative, millions of lives were saved in Africa. In a Rolling Stone article, Bono recalled, "Different political views and whatever. I was the guy who had to come into the office and get him to look up from his big oak table, there in the Oval Office, to let his values tell him what to do." President Bush did just that! He let his values make the decision. And so he teamed up with a pop star and a pop star teamed up with a Republican! Why? The value of human life took priority. So as Green Day wrote an album against President Bush called "Great American Idiot," Bono put differences aside, and they saved actual human lives together!

What do you value? What are your priorities in life? How could these values and priorities take the stress out of the decision-making process? I value my wife, she is a priority and I am committed to her. I do not have daily stress trying to figure out who to date. I have a forever date with my wife. Are your values and priorities honorable and holy before God? If yes, they become a filter in your life and a way to make decisions. As you make these priority-based decisions, your commitment to Jesus will be on full display. It is a commitment to do life with God's heart and His way.

INGREDIENT #4: HEART

Let not steadfast love and faithfulness forsake you;
bind them around your neck; write them on the
tablet of your heart.

"God sees hearts as we see faces." **George Herbert**

I have always been told that "I have a big heart." Heart and passion go hand in hand with me. The 'right' heart fuels great passion. When my heart is off, my passion is off. The heart is where we battle with God. The heart is the core of our being. The heart is what God is after. The heart is what man is after. We want to get to the "heart of the issue." We are told to "follow your heart." We will look to God and flippantly (at times) say, "God knows my heart." Yet, God says through Jeremiah, "The heart is deceitful above all things, and desperately sick; who can understand it?" (Jeremiah 17:9). This is my issue; I follow my heart, all while needing to check my heart. In the next chapter, I'll tell you about the dark times I had in my college years wandering from God. Have I graduated? No. My heart issues have been elevated. The lyrics from "Come Now Fount" reign true in my life even to this day, "prone to wander Lord, I feel it, prone to leave the God I love."

I am a Pharisee. Those four words are not easy to write. The truth is, those four words describe my sinful nature. In speaking to the Pharisees Jesus said in Matthew 15:7-9, "You hypocrites! Well did Isaiah prophesy of you, when he said, 'These people honor me with their lips, but their heart is far from me; in vain do they worship me, teaching as doctrines the commandments of men.'" I do not know if this is theologically accurate, but it describes my feelings; I have grown into this nature. I used to be hot and cold. There was no faking it. When I was on, I was on, when I was off I was off. Now my battle is doing the right thing for the right reasons. As a fleshly Pharisee, I battle a judgmental and condemning spirit. As a fleshly Pharisee, my sin is "better" than others' sin. As a fleshly Pharisee, I have learned how to look good without being good.

Prior to the pandemic many of my habits were the same as they are now. Then and now, I woke up around 4:15 AM. Then and now, I worked out for about an hour a day. Then and now, I had good discipline in my eating. Then and now, I had dedicated times of prayer. Then and now, I had healthy habits outside my professional work. Then and now, I worked 50-60 hours a week. Then and now, I would strive to be a good man for my family. Then and now, I cared very much about being the same man at home as the man I presented myself to be when preaching. So, if old me and new me have many of the same habits, what is the difference? Heart. If the disciples and Pharisees from a religious standpoint looked very similar, what was the difference? Heart.

2020 rocked my habits and forced me to find myself. I thrive with consistently strong habits. I have an addictive personality. When my ability to have consistent habits is hindered, I have difficulty being all in. So, when all was stripped away, I had to find myself. I had to search my heart.

I learned two heart lessons through the pandemic that get at my fleshly Pharisaical heart. The first lesson came one morning when I woke up early to hit the gym. While at the gym, I listened to Gordon Macdonald's "Ordering Your Private World." I was listening to this book because through a church split, my elders gave me four areas I needed to grow in; "Be aware of insecurities and how they play out, feeling the need to control the situation, an intense drive for tangible results." I needed my private life to deal with my insecurities rather than having my professional life exposing my insecurities. There, MacDonald challenged his readers to incorporate times of silence in their private time with God. True, unadulterated silence. No talking, just focused silence.

So when I got home, I decided I would give this a try. I grabbed my dog and we went on my prayer walk. Daily habit. Usually, I spend the time praying as we walk. This morning I prayed and then committed to walking in silence before the Lord. So I walked. No music. No Bible reading playing in my earbuds. Silence. I got to the bay at the end of the road. I watched the sunrise and then started to head back, still in silence. As I walk back my dog has this thing where he walks up to me looking for some love, to chase and be chased. Why then? Who knows? He's a dog. Right after chasing my dog a little bit, after he "got my attention," I audibly yelled at God. "Seriously, no talking? I am wasting time." Right then and there I was wrecked. God answered back, "Jason, I am everywhere, I do not need you to be doing things for me to see you. I always notice and am aware of you." The impression God rocked me with could only have happened through silence. An impression God put on me as my dog "fought" for my attention. I can just be before God and still be noticed by God. Pausing the grind is OK! I do not have to 'accomplish' to be seen. Our God commanded rest, so we accomplish as we rest.

Secondly, I learned that spiritually everyone is different. I knew this but did not lead like I knew this. Spiritual walks will have some similarities but will not all look the same. God has made us all different. My heart is in a bad place when I demand people live out my version of Christianity. My heart is in a bad place when I focus on a change of action before a change of heart. My heart is in a bad place when I am focused on guiding people to be more like me rather than more like Jesus. How a spiritual truth plays out in my life is not always the same way the spiritual truth plays out in your life. I like to buy a $5 gift card when I go to Walmart and give it to a stranger with a "God Loves You" card (provided through our church, which shares the gospel). But to demand that of others? Pharisee. With pastoral guidance, I can encourage and instruct my people to be kind, but with the understanding that kindness will play out differently in each of our lives. These are two key heart issues I learned about myself through the pandemic.

What is Biblical success? *Biblical success is when God's heart and God's ways become my heart and my way.* This last ingredient is essential, as it is a key part of our definition. But it is also at the core of what happens to us through Christ Jesus. "And I will give you a new heart, and a new spirit I will put within you. And I will remove the heart of stone from your flesh and give you a heart of flesh." (Ezekiel 36:26). This is the heart of God, that being, we have a new heart. A heart like our God's.

God's <u>Heart</u> and God's Way

16 From now on, therefore, we regard no one according to the flesh. Even though we once regarded Christ according to the flesh, we regard him thus no longer. 17 Therefore, if anyone is in Christ, he is a new creation. The old has passed away; behold, the new has come. 18 All this is from God, who through Christ reconciled us to himself and gave us the ministry of reconciliation; 19 that is, in Christ God was reconciling the world to himself, not counting their trespasses against them, and entrusting to us the message of reconciliation. 20 Therefore, we are ambassadors for Christ, God making his appeal through us. We implore you on behalf of Christ, be reconciled to God. 21 For our sake he made him to be sin who knew no sin, so that in him we might become the righteousness of God. 2 Corinthians 5:16-21

What I alluded to earlier, I now state clearly: You can look like a new creation without being a new creation. This is the most essential ingredient in the whole recipe. We can do our religious acts of love, but we are still filthy without a new heart. We can act religiously faithful, but without a new heart, we are still filthy. We can be religiously committed, but without a new heart, we are still filthy. Isaiah 64:6 says, "We have all become like one who is unclean, and all our righteous deeds are like a polluted garment. Like the wind, we all fade like a leaf, and our iniquities take us away." Some translations refer to polluted garments as filthy rags.

The heart, when missing from the recipe, may come out looking the same but surely will not taste right. It may "plate" the same, but it won't taste the same. I love my mom's Thanksgiving stuffing. It is not hard to make. Stouffer's stuffing with one added ingredient, sausage! So good. My mom makes killer taco meat. The secret ingredient, ketchup! I make some amazing cookies. But that one time I left out the butter I had put in the microwave to soften, yikes! They looked the same, but that very important ingredient made my cookies taste "filthy," to use that language! When these all-important ingredients are missing, the product is below average and no one worships the cook.

The goal of the gospel and the goal of Scripture all have the same end: worship. David says in Psalm 86:12, "I give thanks to you, O Lord my God, with my whole heart, and I will glorify your name forever." This book has one goal, to help people live lives of worship. Worship is when we take our filthy garments and put on garments of righteousness. We worship anytime we are ascribing God worth indeed, thought, or action from a heart that longs to please Him.

2 Corinthians 5:16-21 is critical to our understanding as it shares the heart of God. It reminds us of the new heart we have received in Christ. For some, maybe you have gotten to this point in the book saying, "Yup, I do that. Check. I do that, check. And that, check. I do all the right things but still, what is missing?" Perhaps you and I share this in common, we are prone to a Pharisaical, religious approach to Christianity. So, whether this is a reminder or a fresh perspective for the very religious among us, let's unpack this passage written by the Pharisees of Pharisees, who became a new creation— the Apostle Paul.

First, let's start in the book of Philippians to see why Paul is a fitting example of a new heart leading to a faithful and successful life towards God.

4 though I have a reason for confidence in the flesh also. If anyone else thinks he has reason for confidence in the flesh, I have more: 5 circumcised on the eighth day, of the people of Israel, of the tribe of Benjamin, a Hebrew of Hebrews; as to the law, a Pharisee; 6 as to zeal, a persecutor of the church; as to righteousness under the law, blameless. 7 But whatever gain I had, I counted as loss for the sake of Christ. 8 Indeed, I count everything as loss because of the surpassing worth of knowing Christ Jesus my Lord. For his sake I have suffered the loss of all things and count them as rubbish, in order that I may gain Christ 9 and be found in him, not having a

righteousness of my own that comes from the law, but that which comes through faith in Christ, the righteousness from God that depends on faith— 10 that I may know him and the power of his resurrection, and may share his sufferings, becoming like him in his death, 11 that by any means possible I may attain the resurrection from the dead. Philippians 3:4-11

What do you see there? You see a man talking about his old life. It was a life with MUCH success. In his religious field, he was as successful as they come. And Paul is now looking back and saying all I gained is loss in light of what I have gained in Christ Jesus. None of that matters! I have gained Jesus. I know Jesus. I know the surpassing worth of Jesus. All that old stuff? Rubbish. The righteousness I produced? Rubbish. I have righteousness from God! How? Through faith in Jesus Christ and His resurrection.

Ok, now we understand the man who is writing, so back to 2 Corinthians 5. The person of Jesus Christ has radically changed Paul. The old him, as successful in the eyes of the world as one could be, still needed a Savior. If the very successful old Paul could not save himself then it must be considered a loss. New Paul? New Paul has gained Jesus! The old Paul looked to his works (the flesh) to feel successful. Not anymore; the new Paul looks to Christ to understand success.

Whom He has gained has now become his ministry. Google defines reconciliation as the "restoration of friendly relations." Old Paul, religiously "perfect" as we have seen, was on bad terms with God. Paul still had sin. The success Paul was experiencing, God did not see as success. When Christ knocked him off his donkey, He said, "Saul (also known as Paul), Saul why are you persecuting Me" (Acts 9:4B). The old Paul who felt successful before God was actually persecuting the Son of God. Well, that is never something we should be successful in! But in Christ, having accepted all that Christ has done, Paul experienced reconciliation. He persecuted the Son of God, but when he accepted the Son of God he was restored to friendly relations with Him! This experience has become his ministry. That is God's heart for humanity. He wants reconciliation for all those who throw hate at His Son. I have a kid, it would take a lot for me to have that heart. God's heart? He "so loved the world He gave His only Son, that whoever believes in Him should not perish but have eternal life." (John 3:16). The heart of God is love for you and I.

The end of 2 Corinthians 5 displays God's heart for us! His heart to send Jesus, along with the actions of Jesus, made a way for Him to extend forgiveness. It made a way for God to justify not counting our sins against us. Jesus lived the perfect life we could not live. He died the death we should have died. This is the beauty of the theological term *imputation*. Imputation happens when something becomes something apart from anything it has done. Let's use the verse to explain. "God made Him who knew no sin, to be sin." Sin was imputed onto Christ. Had Christ sinned? No. He was made to be sin. God imputed all our sins onto Christ. He took our sins and put it on Christ. The perfect became imperfect. Why? So there would be a way for imputation to work in reverse! "So we might become the righteousness of God." Paul was seen as righteous! Wait! The dude that killed Christians, persecuting Christ Himself? Yes. Why? Jesus. Jason is seen as righteous. The dude that has broken all the Ten Commandments in his heart? Yes. Why? Jesus. As sin was taken off of me and put on Christ, righteousness can be taken off Jesus and put on me! It can be, but it is not a guarantee. What a powerful opportunity and act of love given to humanity. He made a way, through faith in Jesus Christ, for us to be reconciled to Him and experience the righteousness of God. To be seen as perfect before God. Oh, what a Savior.

Has the stain of sin been removed from your life? You can be as successful as the old Paul, rising in the ranks, but if you have not accepted Jesus, your life will be a life of rubbish. I do not want to look back on my life and think "rubbish." Romans 10:9-10 says, "because, if you confess with your mouth that Jesus is Lord and believe in your heart that God raised him from the dead, you will be saved. 10 For with the heart one believes and is justified, and with the mouth, one confesses and is saved." This is the way forward. Do you believe Jesus Christ lived perfectly, died in your place and then rose from the grave? Yes? Have you told Him? Have you accepted this gift? Do you understand the heart of God for you? Jesus, the only perfect Person to walk this earth, was the only fitting sacrifice for you and I. God loved us enough to send Him to us. Jesus loved us enough to accomplish the mission. The Holy Spirit loves us enough to guide us forward with the message of reconciliation to the broken world around us. If you have never taken this gift, stop now. Pray: "God, why you love me to send your Son for me, I do not know. God, I have sinned against You. God, I ask your forgiveness through Jesus Christ. I believe He died for me. I believe You rose Him from the grave to give me life. Thank you for this gift. I accept the forgiveness offered through Jesus in faith. Help me to become more like Your perfect Son as I move forward. Amen." Praying this in faith, you share the heart of God. Now let's go live it out!

7 Marks of Someone Successful in the Area of Heart

Repentance and Confession

I have the righteousness of Christ, yet I still sin. You too? As a Christian, I still break the heart of God. Love for Jesus drives my brokenness over sin. If I understand my sin and what it cost my Savior, it must break me. If I understand how offensive sin is to God, it must break me. If it does not, do I know the heart of God? If we know God's love for us and His desire to forgive, we must come humbly before the throne, broken and contrite. 1 John 1:9 says, "If we confess our sins, he is faithful and just to forgive us our sins and to cleanse us from all unrighteousness." Think about this verse lived out. To confess is to name the sin. God already knows what we have done but there is something about articulating it to God. If we have a proper view of God, this is a more harrowing experience than telling our mamas we ain't so innocent! We go before God naming our sin: "God, I looked at that website again." "God, I spent my tithe on Amazon." "God, I threw my kids' food across the kitchen when he refused to eat." "God, I needlessly lied to my wife about where I was going." "God, I think about punching that elder and have cursed him out in my thinking." Confession should be hard. It should impact us. This process should remind us that there is still a process going on in us, and we have not arrived at Christlikeness. Not even close! Ok, that is our part. What is His part? It is said as a promise. Confess your sin properly, and He is faithful to forgive. He is faithful to cleanse. To cleanse is to make perfect again. It is to take the dirty and make it clean. I am dirty and must be 'taken to the Cleaner.' I can be clean through confession and the work Christ does. The heart of God is that when we humbly confess our sins, He is faithful to forgive. When our renewed heart meets God's heart through confession, we will find forgiveness and cleansing. Praise God!

A person who shares the heart of God will repent of sin while confessing sin. They will seek to live as if Jesus were living their life. When we are out of step with Jesus, we bring our sins to God, understanding His heart to forgive. We are committed to life change because our lives must change if we hope to become more like His Son! A person who shares a heart for God will confess their sin when their heart is out of step with God. This is how we experience heart realignment.

Forgiveness

Forgiveness is the mother of all F-words. As a church, we did a series called "F-bomb." Please hold your comments, I have already heard them and know the special place in hell awaiting me (so I have been told) ha! This series was very intentional. We did it over Christmas because around Christmas, we find ourselves in circles that will remind us of forgiveness yet to be extended. That uncle we see but once a year. The friend we have not spoken with since June is at the Christmas party. The person I have wronged and who still will not talk with me will be at the work party. So, the series was called "F-bomb" with the tagline "Forgive or Fracture." We called our people to make a choice: forgive or leave things fractured. It was a powerful series.

Have you heard these quotes before? "To forgive is to set a prisoner free and discover that the prisoner was you." Lewis B Smedes. Or, "Not forgiving someone is like drinking poison and expecting the other person to die" (accredited to a handful of people). Forgiveness is hard. Forgiveness forces us to re-open wounds we are trying to bury. Forgiveness opens us up to being hurt again. Paul wrote in Ephesians 4:32: "Be kind to one another, tenderhearted, forgiving one another, as God in Christ forgave you." In the context of what we are writing about, Christ's heart is a forgiving heart. You have experienced the benefit of a heart of forgiveness. If you are cultivating the heart of God, you must extend forgiveness to those who have wronged you.

Forgiveness perhaps is one of the most authentic ways to express your heart for God. A little bit ago I had to go through a process like this. I experienced deep church hurt. We had a church split. I had people call me a heretic. I had people who were grievance-gathering, holding hurt in their hearts, never letting me know, and then exploding on me. One Saturday, I had someone in my kitchen laughing and joking, only to write a letter to our elders trying to get me fired on Tuesday. I had people damning me for their application of Scripture, not Scripture itself. I had someone spreading a rumor my wife and I were getting a divorce that many took seriously. I had people manipulate or lie about things I had said (or had not said). I was hurt. I was angry. If I am honest, forgiveness felt like an f-word when my heart wanted to use the actual f-word on people. Real talk.

This verse in Ephesians took me on a journey. I met with my mental health counselor and asked him how to go about the process of forgiveness. We set up that process and then I got a group of pastors from around the country to hold me accountable. Here is how it went. One morning I took my prayer walk with my dog to the bay with a backpack. I filled the backpack with rocks. As I sat there, I used a sharpie to write down every name of people (or groups of people) whom I felt had wronged me. I put it in my bag and walked home. It was heavy, as the burden of holding on to unforgiveness is. The next day I started journaling about my major failures in life. I started journaling about my recent failures in life. I started journaling about the forgiveness I had received and was receiving. I could not take rocks out of the bag until I had fully grasped my sin and the forgiveness of God in light of that sin. Then, day by day, I would take a name out of the bag and journal about that person. Each time I would walk through these few steps: (1) Name my sin against that person (2) Name their sin against me (3) How can I show compassion, kindness, and understanding? (4) How can you release yourself from their opinion by elevating God's opinion? (5) Rewrite the Ephesians verse (6) Commit to forgiving the person; writing down my prayer for them (7) Throw the rock into the water, releasing both parties in my heart. Did it fix everything right away? Of course not! It is a process, and it continues to be a process. This exercise became foundational to the journey: I am still on. In the back of that journal, I started writing about what I was learning about forgiveness. I knew this process would teach me, through experience, aspects I had not previously realized. Here are some of the things I wrote (written unedited as I wrote them in my journal);

"God is quick with forgiveness."

"The gap between my 'goodness' and the person who wronged me is not nearly as vast as the gap between me and God. Yet He forgives me wholly, completely, graciously, and quickly."

"You sorry? Yup. Here's the Kingdom."

"The process of forgiveness will require pain, especially emotional, as it did with Jesus."

"God forgave me and loved me before I even knew or understood my sin."

"God doesn't bless feelings as much as He blesses obedience. Obey in forgiveness."

"His list of unforgivable sins is, thankfully, a whole lot shorter than mine."

"Pharisees hated sin and people. Jesus hates sin but loves people. Forgiveness flows from love. Be like Jesus."

"Christ has never abandoned me. Christ says I am worthy. How do I know? Forgiveness. Go and do likewise."

Forgiveness is the hardest thing in the world to process through in Christ-likeness. Yet, this may be the best way to demonstrate a heart entirely devoted to God.

Growing Love

This was a mark we listed in chapter one. There we identified how to be loving. I can look at the moment before me, and choose to love in the moment. But Jesus did not die to have a few select moments of our life. He died so we would be wholly devoted to Him. This is a battle of the heart each and every day. Will you love? And dare I say, will you be increasingly loving? 1 Corinthians 13 is a chapter we have looked to for an understanding of love. The chapter ends by saying, "So now faith, hope, and love abide, these three; but the greatest of these is love." Love is the most significant aspect of the Christian life.

Paul said in Ephesians 3:17-19:

> **17 so that Christ may dwell in your hearts through faith—that you, being rooted and grounded in love, 18 may have the strength to comprehend with all the saints what is the breadth and length and height and depth, 19 and to know the love of Christ that surpasses knowledge, that you may be filled with all the fullness of God.**

When we have the heart of Christ, through faith in Christ, we are rooted and grounded in love. We are to *be* love. Paul is praying for them to have a growing understanding of Christ's love for us. It is a love so vast that we can never fully comprehend its depth. That is a deep love! My kids understand I love them, but do they? Throughout their lives they will *grow* in understanding. When they get married, have kids themselves, when they find themselves as parents in similar situations they were in growing up, they will then grow in understanding how much we loved them. We do this with God as we experience life, as we forgive other people, as we obey, as we pursue humility, as we turn the other cheek, and as we live as Christ lived. We grow in an understanding of His love for us. This then turns into a growing expression of love.

Paul bluntly stated this in Galatians 5:6 when he said, "For in Christ Jesus neither circumcision nor uncircumcision counts for anything, but only faith working through love." A faith expressed in love is all that counts! And this must be a growing love!

> **It is right for me to feel this way about you all, because I hold you in my heart, for you are all partakers with me of grace, both in my imprisonment and in the defense and confirmation of the gospel. 8 For God is my witness, how I yearn for you all with the affection of Christ Jesus. 9 And it is my prayer that your love may abound more and more, with knowledge and all discernment, 10 so that you may approve what is excellent, and so be pure and blameless for the day of Christ, 11 filled with the fruit of righteousness that comes through Jesus Christ, to the glory and praise of God."**
> Philippians 1:7-11

Paul deeply loved the Philippian church. You see that in the opening verses. They held a special place in Paul's heart. Who holds a special place in your heart? How do you pray for them? This verse serves as a litmus test to see if I love people the way God loves them. The first place I must look is how I am praying for them. We will dig into this towards the end of this section, but for our purposes here, look at how Paul is not praying. He is not praying for things. He is not praying for health. There is a time and place for these prayers. Yet here, Paul, who has acknowledged he is praying from his heart, is praying their love may abound. He is praying for the growth of knowledge. He is praying for growing discernment. More to come on the aspect of prayer, but for now, if Paul is praying from the overflow of His heart seeing this as necessary for people he dearly loved, why would it not be true of us as individuals?

Are we growing in love? If yes, your increased knowledge should lead to greater love. Your increased discernment should lead to a holier life where you obey Christ, discerning His will, and all are motivated by love. When will growth no longer be needed? Glory. (Philippians 3:20-21, 1 Thessalonians 5:23). When you and I reach heaven, we will be made perfect. Here this is an everyday battle of sanctification. A heart for Jesus longs to be more like Jesus. Whoever is reading the words I am currently typing, share something with the writer; we both have a long way to go to be more like Jesus. As the elementary school kids' report card will read, "improvement needed," you and I wake up every morning with "improvement needed." A heart for Jesus will take this challenge on the daily. Jesus said, "You shall love the Lord your God with all your heart and with all your soul and with all your mind." (Matthew 27:37). Everyday we want to be growing closer and closer to "all."

Generosity

Money. Another litmus test to see the condition of one's heart is the financial test. The last area we tend to turn over to God is our wallet. This is giving God actual money. We will say, "well, the Old Testament talked about tithes, the New Testament does not." Ok, cool, does your giving communicate worship to the King? "There are other ways to give, I give my time and talents." Ok, cool. Does your bank account communicate worship to the King? "If I am honoring Christ with my finances, ultimately is none of your business." Does your giving communicate you are committed to the King's 'business?'

In the American culture we love privacy and outing people. We love to keep private what we want to keep private, while trying to make videos we hope will go viral. We pick and choose what we want to be known and what is "not your business." This has become the way of the church and is best seen in the area of finances. Pastors are allowed to hold people accountable in every area but finances. Why? Does holiness matter in every area but finances? And yes, I hear what you are already saying, "pastors are not perfect. The church has a history of abuse." Go to a church that has learned from past mistakes, and build God's kingdom there. Stop making every excuse under the sun not to give. This is a heart issue. Those with a heart issue in giving will make any excuse they can not to give. Those with a heart to give, look for areas to build God's kingdom with their finances.

The New Testament examples of giving far exceed 10%. In Luke 21, the widow gave out of her poverty. Arguably, this was all she had. It was closer to 100% than it was to 10%. In Acts 2 and 4, we see the extreme giving of the gospel-believing community. They sold homes, land, and shared possessions, all to help people. Giving was ingrained in them as a part of life. In one section, it seems they often gave 100% (Acts 4:36-37). So, yes, I agree with you; the New Testament does not mandate an amount of money to give. The New Testament anticipates your finances to be an area in which the love of Christ is put on display. In Christ, we have been freed from the love of money (1 Timothy 6:10), allowing money to become an area where we can communicate worth to Christ.

> **6 The point is this: whoever sows sparingly will also reap sparingly, and whoever sows bountifully will also reap bountifully. 7 Each one must give as he has decided in his heart, not reluctantly or under compulsion, for God loves a cheerful giver.** 2 Corinthians 9:6-7

What has your heart decided to give? What is the attitude in which you give? What do your finances communicate you worship? Does the margin you wish you had get eaten up by things of this world or the world to come? Are your finances building your kingdom or His kingdom? Do you give God your first fruits, or are you content giving Him last fruits (leftovers)? If God loves a cheerful giver, then this is what I want to strive to be. All I have is Yours, Jesus. I can't take any of it with me, so take it and use it. It comes from you, and it is yours to use. Have a plan and work on the plan. Plan to give. Decide to give. Do so with joy. Pick a percentage right now and start there. Percentage giving is the decision. "God, I have decided I will give You 5% of whatever I make." Then do some math and it is decided! As you abound in love, can you abound in giving? As your income increases, don't raise your standard of living, raise your standard of giving. In percentage giving, the amount grows as your income grows.

Our finances were all over the place for my wife and me in our early years of marriage. My mom and dad visited once, and you know how much was in our bank account to put food on the table? $9. Nothing else until payday the next day. Somehow we made it work, but it was not sustainable. We started following Dave Ramsey's financial steps to freedom. We created a monthly budget. We stuck to it. We began to pay off all our school debt. It was a ten-year battle. We wanted financial freedom so we could be increasingly generous. This was always the heart we would project to each other and friends in prayer.

In May of 2021, this was tested. The following month, June, we were finally going to be debt free minus the house. Then one Sunday we got the news that a younger friend in ministry was in a car accident. He was fine, but his car was not. He was in town to take his mom's car, and that car got totaled during the visit. He needed a vehicle very quickly. A GoFundMe was set up for him. Ava came to me that Sunday afternoon and told me all about the situation. I could tell she wanted us to do something, so I said, "I mean I guess we can give $200 to the GoFundMe." It was not good enough. She wanted to give him our Toyota Corolla. I quickly looked up the value and said, "we can sell our car for $7,250; we are not giving away our car!" We were a month away from being debt free minus the house; this would put us back a full year. We walked away from the casual conversation and just prayed about it.

The next day, I was doing my morning devotions, and I could not help this feeling that I needed to give him our car. I was convicted that I wanted the title of debt-free minus the house more than I wanted to be generous. I was reminded of everything I had told others about sacrifice, love, the cost of following Jesus, and things of that nature. As I prayed for this young man, I knew I had the means to help. The book of James talks about offering people nice thoughts but not doing anything about it (James 2:16). My heart was tested, and my initial response was not good. Through time with God, my heart was being transformed into Christ's heart.

So, Ava and I quickly decided on the car we wanted to replace her car with (this is the car she drives for work). Would you know, the local dealership just so happened to have the exact car we wanted in stock that day?! I went that morning and bought a brand-new car. On the way, I prayed, "God, please allow us to be debt free minus the house, paying off this car in one year."

Now follow me here. Ava and I had a plan on how we would spend our extra monthly income when we paid off our debt. We planned on putting an additional $300 toward our mortgage. Keep this in mind. The week after giving away our car, I decided to refinance our home, trying to get us towards that debt free minus the house position. A month into the refinance process, I asked them if we could add the cost of our car to the refinance. They said yes, but it would raise our monthly bill by $300. When the refinance went through, I had a new work car for my wife (a newer car), 12 years knocked off my mortgage, and no change to our financial plan! My monthly overhead remained the same. We were debt free minus the house. I ended the year in a better financial situation than I could have imagined in May. It was all sparked by giving away a car worth $7,250. Only God.

Worship

Christian worship is ultimately about ascribing God worth. Giving God time in the morning to focus my day ascribes God worth. When giving 10%+ to the local church does not make financial sense, I ascribe God worth because it makes spiritual sense. When the talents he has given me can be used to build my net worth, but I use them to build His kingdom, I ascribe Him worth. As we just said, do your finances communicate worth to God? Does your calendar and how you spend your time communicate worth to God? Obeying God is a heart issue. Those who long for God long to do the will of God. Choosing to obey God ascribes Him worth because we communicate that "of the two ways before me, I choose Your way, Jesus."

When we live like this, we make our lives an act of worship. Romans 12:1-2 says:

> **I appeal to you, therefore, brothers, by the mercies of God, to present your bodies as a living sacrifice, holy and acceptable to God, which is your spiritual worship. 2 Do not be conformed to this world, but be transformed by the renewal of your mind, that by testing you may discern what is the will of God, what is good and acceptable and perfect.**

This requires sacrifice. Daily. It requires us to choose Jesus and not this world, decision by decision. This requires us to make God's voice the loudest voice in our heads. This requires us to make the Holy Spirit the greatest influence in our lives. As we live like this, we ascribe God worth. We say in our actions, "your way is the best way." Easy to write, proclaim and sing on a Sunday morning, but hard to do in reality. Why? God's way will require you to forgive, turn the other cheek, give financially, go to church instead of watching online, read your Bible when you want to sleep a little more, work on the cussing problem, invest in your marriage when it gets hard, etc. A heart that longs for Jesus will long to live like Jesus to the point of actionable change. This is transformation. Google defines transformation as *"a thorough or dramatic change in form or appearance."* Every day we worship God by choosing to become more like His Son. A change of heart leads to a changed way of living.

A changed life produced by the changed heart we have received is what Christ will look for when we meet Him. As Christ has given all of Himself to us, did our lives become a life of worship to the King? We cannot answer yes merely because we sang 3-4 'worship' songs a few times a month at church. Without heart change leading to life change, our worship services are full of lip service. This is nothing new;

> **You hypocrites! Well did Isaiah prophesy of you, when he said: 8 "'These people honor me with their lips, but their heart is far from me; 9 in vain do they worship me, teaching as doctrines the commandments of men.'"** Matthew 15:8-9

9 With it we bless our Lord and Father, and with it we curse people who are made in the likeness of God. 10 From the same mouth come blessing and cursing. My brothers, these things ought not to be so. James 3:9-10

A heart in full service to the King will transcend lip service. Sing songs of praise to the King and curse at our kids on the way home, "these things ought not to be so." Sing of giving God all of ourselves, while never financially contributing to His church, "these things ought not to be so." Praising the holiness of God while never cracking open our Bible during the week, "these things ought not to be so." We could go on and on. The point remains, Christ gave all of Himself for all of you. Worship Him with your whole heart, giving Him your whole life.

Gratitude

This is hard. Ya. Jesus didn't give all of Himself, so we could sit back and eat cupcakes all day! When we focus on how hard it is, religion slowly creeps in. We begin saying, "I have to over and over again." I have to read my Bible. I have to go to church. I have to stop drinking. I have to be faithful to my spouse.' I have to… The "I have to" life flows out of the ungrateful life.

Three passages stop me in my tracks every time I read them:

The Lord your God is in your midst, a mighty one who will save; he will rejoice over you with gladness; he will quiet you by his love; he will exult over you with loud singing. Zephaniah 3:17

See what kind of love the Father has given to us, that we should be called children of God; and so we are. The reason why the world does not know us is that it did not know him. 1 John 3:1

Come now, let us reason together, says the Lord: though your sins are like scarlet, they shall be as white as snow; though they are red like crimson, they shall become like wool. Isaiah 1:18

These verses rock me every time I come to them. If cancel culture wants to come knocking at my door, they can. I said "acceptable" things in the culture I grew up in. These statements now shame me. Remember that forgiveness journey I mentioned? I started by journaling how I was a man in need of forgiveness and concluded with "I am a worthless piece of crap." No one on planet earth is more undeserving of forgiveness than the man who types these words. And then I read Zephaniah 3. What? The Lord of all is "glad" I exist? Rejoices over me? Sings over me? Wants to quiet me with His love? How can this be?! What love! Then I read 1 John 3 and what? I am a child of God? He looks at me as a son. He looks at me with greater love than I have for my own kids? I am not just accepted, I am FAMILY! What love! I read Isaiah 1 and I am fully aware that my sin dirties all that is pure white. I get that imagery. And yet, clean. My Jesus makes me CLEAN. What love!

What love indeed. "I have to" is not a fitting response for the one who understands the great love Christ has poured on us. I love my wife. She loves me. We are in a love relationship. The other day I did something small, but for her, it meant so much. She was working early in the morning, so I threw an English muffin in the toaster and poured a cup of coffee. Then after putting some peanut butter on that English muffin, I brought it to her desk. She was so thankful. To respond with, "you're my wife; I had to." Welp, that would have taken a really good thing and turned it into a really bad thing. Why? Bad heart. But to respond, "you're my wife, I get to love you," reveals a heart of gratitude.

We love out of an overflow of the love we have received. Jesus said in John 13:34, "A new commandment I give to you, that you love one another: just as I have loved you, you also are to love one another." You do not have to love others, you respond to Christ's love by loving others. With free will in play, this is a voluntary response to what Christ has done for us. Andy Stanley says, "We don't obey to gain anything. We obey because of all we have already gained."[1] Paul writes in Ephesians 5 that as dearly loved children we are to walk the way of love. When we love those around us, motivated by the love of Christ, we are living a life of worship. Love as a response to all God has done for us in Christ Jesus is worship. It flows from a heart that has

---

[1] Stanley, Andy. 2015. *Starting Point Conversation Guide Revised Edition: A Conversation about Faith.* Grand Rapids, MI: Zondervan. Pg.94.

understood, accepted, and been moved by the loving forgiveness Christ has given to us.

Dependency

After college, I moved to Lynchburg, Virginia, to live with my brothers and spend time "finding myself." Spiritually I was far from God. I knew it and needed to return to the person God had called me to be. Spiritually, things got worse before they got better. One New Year's Eve, a girl I was seeing called me up at American Eagle where I worked. The conversation got heated and she yelled, "you can ace any Bible test put before you, but you don't believe a 'darn' word of it." It was as if God reached through the phone and grabbed my beating heart with her words. I had adult smarts without childlike faith.

There are plenty of really smart adults that can ace a Bible test. There were (and are) plenty of Pharisees that knew the Scriptures inside and out, yet had hearts far from God. The Christian with a heart that longs for God will go to God's word and give the Holy Spirit room to bring about life change. With that heart, we become doers of the word as James says (James 1:22-25). The Christian with a heart for God is dependent on God's word. In Acts 17, the Bereans depended on the word of God to see if what they were being taught checked out with God's word. Psalm 119:105 speaks of the word as a lamp for our feet. Ever been overnight hiking without a lamp in the middle of the wilderness? It is a very big deal. It is dangerous. As dangerous as it is for the Christian dependent upon himself to navigate the darkness of this world. In darkness, the Christian is dependent upon illumination and we have it. We have it in the word of God! It shows us when we are off course. A heart that longs for Jesus wants to stay the course. This grows hunger (heart) for God's word.

As I was going through the process of planting Wellspring Church, my denomination provided me with a coach. At the time, I was accustomed to working 60-75 hours a week. During my church planter assessment, a week where ministry professionals drill you to see if you are called to church planting, this was a big red flag they heard from me and felt from my wife. They saw the gifting, but also saw someone relying on their own strength.

This information was passed along to my church planting coach. During one of our sessions, we read Hebrews 4 together. It is a section on Sabbath rest. He then looked up and said, "Jason, are you willing to obey God?" That was it. The question rocked me. Simply reading God's word and a challenge to be obedient. I wasn't obedient. A day off? That is for the lazy, so I thought. Not when God commands it! The world does not depend on me. It depends on God. Sabbath is proof you rely on Jesus and desire unadulterated time with Him.

The Jesus we are dependent upon is the Jesus we pray to. At my former church, one of our values was prayer and our tagline was "an expression of dependency." If I can handle life on my own, I do not need prayer. But since God has not designed life to be that way, I need prayer because I need the God behind prayer. Like we said, prayer is like a walkie-talkie for soldiers on the front lines. We are those soldiers on a mission, on the front lines. We have a powerful device in our hands to radio home base and call in the bombs, planes and reserves. Do you not know the necessity of prayer because you are not on the front lines? Get off the sidelines and get to the front lines. Here you will understand what dependent prayer is all about.

Earlier, we looked at Philippians 1:7-11. Paul longed for people to grow in their relationship with Christ. He longed to see them have a love for Christ that abounds more and more. Paul knew he could give people tools. He could have expressed what our motivation should be. However, Paul goes to prayer because that is all he can do. Shaping and breaking a heart happens through the power of the Spirit. Man cannot do this. God may use the words of a man, but it is still a work of God. So Paul went to God in dependent prayer, begging Him to move in the lives of the people he loved.

Is your heart still self-reliant? Before you answer yes or no, examine how you *personally* handle the scriptures. When was the last time you were convicted and changed something about your life because of what you read in scripture? Examine your sabbath rest. Do you take focused time off to just be with God? Do you say, "I can't," pointing to a life of busyness? When did you become a god with the world revolving around you? Examine your prayer life. Do your prayers express dependency on God? Do they express that you need God for what you are incapable of doing? Now answer the question, is your heart still self-reliant as it was before you said yes to a relationship with Jesus? May our hearts never stop singing, "Oh Lord, I need you, every hour of every day."

The Example of Jesus

This is the most challenging chapter to write because the heart is the core of a person. The heart is what is under fire by the enemy. The heart is where war is raged. Everyday there is a battle for control within your heart that leads to specific outcomes. Your heart produces fruit that, when controlled by Jesus, looks like Jesus. When you do not give control of your heart to Jesus, your fruit does not look holy like Jesus, it looks (is) sinful. The heart is all-consuming. You could say everything we have written up until this point in the book is a matter of the heart. Those who share the heart of the Father will live like His perfect Son. No chapter can adequately capture the all-consuming and all-encompassing nature of one's heart. But starting with what a heart captured by faith in Jesus, then looking at seven key marks of a person who has given their heart to Jesus, we now turn to Jesus, Himself. Will we be able to capture everything about the heart of Jesus? No. In fact, every day we learn more and more about the heart of Jesus, hoping to live it out more and more. Let's start with something Jesus said about the heart, followed by two critical aspects Jesus' heart treasures:

> **19 "Do not lay up for yourselves treasures on earth, where moth and rust destroy and where thieves break in and steal, 20 but lay up for yourselves treasures in heaven, where neither moth nor rust destroys and where thieves do not break in and steal. 21 For where your treasure is, there your heart will be also. 22 "The eye is the lamp of the body. So, if your eye is healthy, your whole body will be full of light, 23 but if your eye is bad, your whole body will be full of darkness. If then the light in you is darkness, how great is the darkness! 24 "No one can serve two masters, for either he will hate the one and love the other, or he will be devoted to the one and despise the other. You cannot serve God and money.** Matthew 6:19-24

What you treasure puts your heart on display. Do you treasure things here on earth that will one day cease to be? Or do you treasure the things of God which are eternal? Who is the master of your heart? God the Father or the lesser gods of this world? What do your eyes gravitate towards? What do your eyes long to see? What is your mind fixated on? Many of the aforementioned marks serve as a litmus test to see if I genuinely treasure God and if my heart longs for God. Personally speaking, they have been key in my life. When my heart is lit on fire for my Jesus, confessing sin, personal repentance, love, generosity, worship, gratitude, and dependency is easier. Note, not easy-easier. When my heart is not on fire for the Lord, personally, these areas become key struggles in my life. I'll give, but reluctantly. I'll forgive in theory but not in spirit. I'll talk a dependent talk without living a dependent walk. I'll sing worship songs while failing to live a life of worship. What are your battles? Where is your heart on full display? God's heart was on full display through Jesus. In this, what did He treasure? Obedience to the Father and love for people.

Now let's examine John 4:1-42. I am going to include the text here. Yes, it is long. Yes, I could tell you to go to your Bible and read it. But when I read and authors tell me to read a passage, I don't. I assume I know it well enough and can fill in the blanks with the author's words. This is too important. Read John 4:1-42. As you read, highlight where you see the Father's heart on display through Jesus.

> **Now when Jesus learned that the Pharisees had heard that Jesus was making and baptizing more disciples than John 2 (although Jesus himself did not baptize, but only his disciples), 3 he left Judea and departed again for Galilee. 4 And he had to pass through Samaria. 5 So he came to a town of Samaria called Sychar, near the field that Jacob had given to his son Joseph. 6 Jacob's well was there; so Jesus, wearied as he was from his journey, was sitting beside the well. It was about the sixth hour. 7 A woman from Samaria came to draw water. Jesus said to her, "Give me a drink." 8 (For his disciples had gone away into the city to buy food.) 9 The Samaritan woman said to him, "How is it that you, a Jew, ask for a drink from me, a woman of Samaria?" (For Jews have no dealings**

with Samaritans.) 10 Jesus answered her, "If you knew the gift of God, and who it is that is saying to you, 'Give me a drink,' you would have asked him, and he would have given you living water." 11 The woman said to him, "Sir, you have nothing to draw water with, and the well is deep. Where do you get that living water? 12 Are you greater than our father Jacob? He gave us the well and drank from it himself, as did his sons and his livestock." 13 Jesus said to her, "Everyone who drinks of this water will be thirsty again, 14 but whoever drinks of the water that I will give him will never be thirsty again. The water that I will give him will become in him a spring of water welling up to eternal life." 15 The woman said to him, "Sir, give me this water so that I will not be thirsty or have to come here to draw water." 16 Jesus said to her, "Go, call your husband, and come here." 17 The woman answered him, "I have no husband." Jesus said to her, "You are right in saying, 'I have no husband'; 18 for you have had five husbands, and the one you now have is not your husband. What you have said is true." 19 The woman said to him, "Sir, I perceive that you are a prophet. 20 Our fathers worshiped on this mountain, but you say that in Jerusalem is the place where people ought to worship." 21 Jesus said to her, "Woman, believe me, the hour is coming when neither on this mountain nor in Jerusalem will you worship the Father. 22 You worship what you do not know; we worship what we know, for salvation is from the Jews. 23 But the hour is coming, and is now here when the true worshipers will worship the Father in spirit and truth, for the Father is seeking such people to worship him. 24 God is spirit, and those who worship him must worship in spirit and truth." 25 The woman said to him, "I know that Messiah is coming (he who is called Christ). When he comes, he will tell us all things." 26 Jesus said to her, "I who speak to you am he." 27 Just then his disciples came back. They marveled that he was talking with a woman, but no one said, "What do you seek?" or, "Why are you talking with her?" 28 So the woman left her water jar and went away into town and said to the people, 29 "Come, see a man who told me all that I ever did. Can this be the Christ?" 30 They went out of the town and were coming to him. **31** Meanwhile the disciples were urging him, saying, "Rabbi, eat." **32** But he said to them, "I have food to eat that you do not know about." **33** So the disciples said to one another, "Has anyone brought him something to eat?" **34** Jesus said to them, "My food is to do the will of him who sent me and to accomplish his work. **35** Do you not say, 'There are yet four months, then comes the harvest'? Look, I tell you, lift up your eyes, and see that the fields are white for harvest. **36** Already the one who reaps is receiving wages and gathering fruit for eternal life, so that sower and reaper may rejoice together. **37** For here the saying holds true, 'One sows and another reaps.' **38** I sent you to reap that for which you did not labor. Others have labored, and you have entered into their labor." **39** Many Samaritans from that town believed in him because of the woman's testimony, "He told me all that I ever did." **40** So when the Samaritans came to him, they asked him to stay with them, and he stayed there two days. **41** And many more believed because of his word. **42** They said to the woman, "It is no longer because of what you said that we believe, for we have heard for ourselves, and we know that this is indeed the Savior of the world." John 4:1-42

I believe there are two critical aspects of the heart of God on full display through this passage; His obedient heart and His heart for people. As His heart is on full display, we see what Christ treasures; obeying His Father and people. The heart pursues treasure and treasures display the heart. In this passage, we see Jesus living out Matthew 22:37-39, where Christ responds to a question about which is the greatest commandment with, "And he said to him, "You shall love the Lord your God with all your heart and with all your soul and with all your mind. **38** This is the great and first commandment. **39** And a second is like it: You shall love your neighbor as yourself." In this passage, we see Christ loving His Father with all His heart, soul, and mind as He is loving His neighbor. Let's examine these two elements.

A Heart that Treasures Obeying God

Jesus, who would not be drawn into even the thought of turf wars with John the Baptist, leaves Judea to head towards Galilee. The shortest route was through Samaria, but the typical route for the average Jew was to avoid Samaria, taking a longer route around this region. Racism, hatred, cruelty, avoidance, and the like were commonplace between the Jews and the Samaritans. Obeying His Father took Jesus places others would avoid. Beyond my childhood, I have never actually followed a map looking for treasure but I imagine this is much the same. When looking for a real treasure chest of gold, you will journey places others naturally avoid. Jesus, with a focus on God and people, *had* to go to Samaria and DID!

Weariness was a byproduct of what he had done. He is tired. It is midday. He is worn out and hot. This will happen as our heart pursues treasure. A treasure that is worth it will make us tired. The pursuit of treasure will push us to exhaustion. So why do it? The treasure is worth it. If the treasure is not worth it, we would never put such effort into the journey. The weariness of Jesus communicates worth. It communicates He willfully pushed Himself to this state to pursue the mission His Father put before Him. Christ treasured obeying His Father and was willing to tire Himself to do so.

Tired people often have a hard time thinking. Google "tired brain" and Google will spit back 326,000,000 responses in less than a second. Jesus, weary from the journey, has seemingly lost His mind. At least that is what the average person would see. We know because it is Jesus, that this is not the case. But for the onlooker, "Jesus, what are you thinking? Talking to a woman? A Samaritan woman? Alone? Showing her respect? Treating her with dignity?" These questions get at social norms Jesus is breaking by having a conversation with this woman. It is what will spark questions from His disciples. Jesus, initially, was misunderstood. He knew it and did not care. If obeying God results in being misunderstood by man, let me be misunderstood all day long! Jesus' heart to obey God led Him to be misunderstood by most. He was ok with it. He embraced it. Some would eventually understand and went on to turn the ancient world upside down with this gospel message! When we cultivate a heart desiring to obey the Father, we will be misunderstood by those that do not share the same heart.

The disciples were beginning to share the heart of Jesus, but it was still in process. So, when they return, they have questions. It is here we see the heart of obedience on full display. Up until this point, we have been looking at signposts that point to this heartbeat. Now, toward the end of the story, Jesus puts the pieces we have looked at together. "**Jesus said to them, "My food is to do the will of him who sent me and to accomplish his work."** (John 4:34). He goes on to say, in essence, "look around, the opportunities are endless. There are opportunities all around us!" Food fuels. What fuels Jesus? Doing the will of God and accomplishing His work. Jesus is stating clearly His motivation. What motivates you is, yet again, a snapshot into your heart. Motivated to make money? Money is a treasure of your heart. Does family motivate you? Family is a treasure of the heart. These motivations are not wrong until they become *the* motivation. These motivations are not bad until they become primary. Jesus is sharing the primary motivation of His heart. He is telling His disciples what ultimately drives Him to do what He does; God's will and accomplishing His work. Desire without action is delusion. Jesus wasn't delusional! He acted on the desires of His heart. How did Jesus accomplish the will of God? How was Jesus obedient? People.

A Heart that Treasures People

"Jesus had to go through Samaria," said no well-meaning Jew ever! But Jesus did. Why? He had a divine appointment with a lady society had disregarded at a well in Samaria. To take the expected route around Samaria would cause Him to miss this appointment. So Jesus had to place Himself in Samaria because that is where He'd find this woman. If Jesus had been into statistics, He would not have done this. On paper, Jesus had great opportunities in the two other regions mentioned, Judea and Galilee. These are the regions Jesus saw crowds. These are the regions where being a Jew at least had some weight. Samaria? Come on, Jesus. It is just simple math. Don't waste your time. Go where there is impact. Go where you can get the biggest bang for your buck, as they say. Nope. God wanted Him to meet this one woman because this one woman mattered. Because she mattered to the Father, she mattered to Jesus. If your heart treasures people, you will journey after all people with a heartbeat. You will not exclude some because you will see all people matter to God and so all people will matter to you.

People matter to God because they are broken, and He alone can "fix broken." With a heart that treasures seeing broken people be made whole, Jesus acknowledges her sin. He makes clear that she's been a little loosiegoosie, if you will. She has not been sexually pure. In fact, when she goes into town, this is what stands out to her. I mean, she likely had a reputation of sexual impurity. So is it weird that she walks into town proclaiming: "come check out this dude that shared with me all I have ever done?" And somehow it worked! This is important, catch this. It worked because Jesus brought her brokenness to the surface to fix her with His grace (living water). He did not bring it to the surface to leave her broken! In meeting her with grace in her brokenness, this became about His love and not her sin. A heart that treasures people will not share the gospel with an either/or strategy, highlighting sin or grace. A heart that treasures people will share the gospel with a both/ and strategy; highlighting both sin and grace. People need the good news of the gospel and they need to understand what makes it good news!

This is somewhat assumed in what was just said, but must be highlighted; a heart that treasures people offers them Jesus. If your heart is all about Jesus and people, your "Jesus heart" will shine when you interact with people. Here, Jesus creates an opportunity to share Himself. He places Himself at a well so He can talk about Himself as living water. Paul did this in Acts 17 when he was in Athens. He saw their statues to gods and specifically the one to an unknown god just in case they missed one. He then uses it to share the gospel, making the unknown Jesus known to them. Paul and Jesus are aware of the environment and use it to declare the gospel. Jesus is the focus. The best thing any of us have to offer people is Jesus. If you treasure someone, do you not give them your very best? Give them Jesus. If you love someone, you cannot help but talk with them. Talk about Jesus. A heart that treasures people, because they treasure Jesus, will shine a light on Jesus.

With Jesus and people as our heartbeat, we push through the weariness of life. My time is always God's time. We will get tired. Jesus got tired. Sit back for a second and think about this. Jesus, being fully man and fully God, was able to be fatigued. He is sitting down by the well because He is weary from the journey. This is humanly understandable. How do you act in a tired and weary state? What is your mental focus? I am not the only human on earth to answer with; "ME! I am my focus when I am tired. I get (more) selfish." Jesus, because of whom and what He treasured, maintains an "others" focus. In fact, He even used His tired state, His tired appearance, to open up the conversation by asking for water. His concern was not the water or what the disciples went into town to get. He was able to push physical weariness aside and focus on this woman. This does not mean we never focus on ourselves. Do not close the book and become a sinful workaholic. What this does mean is that as you have the opportunity, so take it! Seek Christ for strength to accomplish the work of Christ. It means when you are resting, you are resting with a purpose. It is a quick break to get back out there. A heart that treasures people will fight through tired bodies.

As stated, if we treasure people, we treasure all people. This could still mean God would send me to a specific group of people. Paul focused on Gentiles but still preached in synagogues to Jewish people. God can send us to a specific people group, but that never means we forgo sharing the gospel with the person in front of us. Who is in front of Jesus? A very sinful woman with a very known reputation. In that day in age, you were guilty by association. I will state that stronger: You were damned by association. You were seen as unholy not only by what you did but also by who you were with. But as Jesus said in Mark 2:17, He came for the sick, not the healthy. He came not for those that would make Him look holy; He came for the unholy. If you treasure people, do you treasure all people? Are there certain people groups you would be uncomfortable sharing Jesus with? Are there certain social associations you would "feel a way" about associating with? Are there ethnic groups? Is it the LGBTQ+ community? Is it the uncle in your family that no one associates with? Is it the neighbor who has leaves always blowing into your yard? Is it the kid from down the street who is more likely to get egged than invited? Jesus came for all people. Jesus was willing to associate with people in need of grace. THAT IS ALL PEOPLE. "Associate with" does not mean "participate with." Truth is freeing. A heart that treasures people will break down walls to reach all people.

Because this last one is so important, why was it saved for the end? Let me close with this illustration. I used to hang out at a coffee shop owned by a guy who was friendly to our church to make money but was not a Christian. He would do anything to get famous. He craves fame. If a video of him and his 6-year-old daughter cursing would go viral, he is all for it. Exploiting his wife and her body to get the views, he is all for it. Their social media is morally disgusting. But he likes golf. I like golf. He needs Jesus and I know Jesus. So I kept asking him to play golf. Finally, he said yes! Golf is great because it gives me five hours to find gospel opportunities; they are stuck with me! On the 10th hole, we were in the fairway and someone drove on us. This means they teed off, did not wait, and soared a golf ball over our heads. In golf, this is a big deal. He had a decent amount of whisky at this point and lost his crap. He shouted stuff, hit the golf ball back at them, and so on. I, the pastor, who does not drink for personal reasons, sat in the golf cart. I was literally thinking, "what if these guys he's screaming at go to Wellspring or see me and know I am the pastor of Wellspring?" What could it mean for my reputation? I literally felt like running. Until it hit me. If someone wants to ruin my reputation for hanging out with a guy who clearly needs Jesus, so be it. I was not participating in the sinful behavior, I was focused on a person who needs Jesus. Did he accept Christ that day? No. Did he eventually? I honestly do not know and do not see the fruit that he has. He has since moved. But I do know, when life hit the fan for him, he came to me at the coffee shop for perspective because I opened the door relationally and always kept my focus on Jesus. I pray whether today, tomorrow, or in the years to come, God will use these past moments to bring this man to salvation.

Playing golf that day, my heart, intentions and focus truly were on Jesus. I was not looking for a good time, I fought for a "God time." The heart of God desires our worship. Will you worship God through obedience? Obedience will awkwardly bring you to people who make you feel uncomfortable and even sinful. Peter felt sinful when asked to minister to Gentiles. Pharisees saw Jesus as sinful when He ate with sinners. In their minds a man of God would never hang out or associate with the people Jesus associated with. Who was more holy? The Pharisees in their disassociations or Jesus in His associations? Jesus all day long. So will you worship God and obey God by loving people? Will you see the purposes of God, bringing salvation to the nations, as your purpose? Do you share the heart of God by loving the people who have His heart?

What is Biblical success? *Biblical success is when God's heart and God's ways become my heart and my way.* Want to be successful in the eyes of God? Share the heart of the Father as displayed through the Son.

INGREDIENT #4: HEART
BIBLICAL CASE STUDY

Let not steadfast love and faithfulness forsake you;
bind them around your neck; write them on
the tablet of your heart.

"We know the truth, not only by the reason,
but also by the heart." **Blaise Pascal**

*B*iblical success is when God's heart and God's ways become my heart and my way. This side of heaven, we will never fully live this out. We will not obtain perfection in this life. I have failed. I will fail. What is the cry of your heart when you fail? Does failure build upon failure? How does one grow stronger out of failure? These are questions we could all ask ourselves.

David writes in Psalm 51:1-2: "Have mercy on me, O God, according to your steadfast love; according to your abundant mercy blot out my transgressions. Wash me thoroughly from my iniquity, and cleanse me from my sin!" Have you been in this place? A place where you know you have sinned and are wrecked by it? This is not sorrow that I got caught, this is a deep mourning that I have done something ugly. There is no failure like moral failures. There is no failure like sin failure.

Throughout Scripture the heart of David is referenced. Please do not skip over these verses; think about them. Before we get into what David did, we must understand what is said of his heart.

> **14 But now your kingdom shall not continue. The Lord has sought out a man after his own heart, and the Lord has commanded him to be prince over his people, because you have not kept what the Lord commanded you."** 1 Samuel 13:14

> **7 But the Lord said to Samuel, "Do not look on his appearance or on the height of his stature, because I have rejected him. For the Lord sees not as man sees: man looks on the outward appearance, but the Lord looks on the heart."** 1 Samuel 16:7

> **"For when Solomon was old his wives turned away his heart after other gods, and his heart was not wholly true to the Lord his God, as was the heart of David his father."** 1 Kings 11:4

> **And when he had removed him, he raised up David to be their king, of whom he testified and said, 'I have found in David the son of Jesse a man after my heart, who will do all my will.'** Acts 13:22

Saul was replaced because of the heart he lacked. David was seen and promoted for his heart. Solomon would eventually be seen as someone who lacked the heart his father David had. Historically, in Acts, David is remembered for being a man after God's own heart. Great guy with a great heart. Also, a great sinner with an even greater God.

2 Samuel 11 puts on display David's great sin and God's great love. As we walk through what David did, remember the goodness of God that did not destroy David, helped him rebound, and when it all came to an end, saw Him as a "man after God's own heart."

Here, like all of humanity, David fails to seek after God's heart. In a season when kings typically went off to war, David stayed home. David, the warrior, does not join the troops, he's home in the palace for a bit of rest and relaxation. One day he gets up from a midday nap, goes out to his balcony, and sees a woman bathing. To make a long story short, he sees her, takes her, impregnates her, and then via his command, murders her husband who is off fighting. If anyone deserves to be punished, it is David. God sends the Prophet Nathan to confront David in his sin. We are working through David's response to the confrontation of his sin as we wrestle through Psalm 51:

This Psalm is written as a prayer to God. The fact that David is praying is significant. In our brokenness, how many of us feel worthless and run from God. Praying is the last thing we feel like doing and the last thing we feel *worthy* to do. David knows what a close relationship with God looks like. He understands how his sin has destroyed it. He puts no blame on God. He wants this relationship back. He wants the closeness back. It is a plea that has ownership of sin. This plea is filled with hope. Mainly, he hopes forgiveness will be extended and that this will lead to restoration. In the ugliness of our sin, how do we respond? Do we see it as ugly? Do we try to justify it? Do we try to rationalize it? Do we try to redefine sin? Are we trying to remove the guilt of sin while letting sin remain? How we respond to failure, puts our heart on full display. How we respond reveals our heart while simultaneously revealing what we understand of the heart of God.

Shame and sorrow have differences we need to unpack. Shame belongs in the pit of hell. Sorrow is a godly response to sin. As we think about our heart in conjunction with the heart of God, I want us to respond as Christ would want us to respond. When I feel shame, I feel ashamed as I sit in humiliation. Shame paralyzes a person. But the main difference, the focus is on me and what I feel. Sorrow, on the other hand, carries with it a feeling of being ashamed. It has a sense of humiliation. In sorrow, I am disappointed to the point of change. In our context, as it relates to sin (not as it relates to loss), the focus is on whom we have hurt and bettering ourselves in light of that. Shame brings hurt through humiliation, and sorrow brings hurt through what I have done to another. By the end of this chapter, you and I may just begin to grasp that old fuddy-duddy word: contrition- a sorrowful response. David continues on praying in Psalm 51:

For I know my transgressions, and my sin is ever before me. Against you, you only, have I sinned and done what is evil in your sight, so that you may be justified in your words and blameless in your judgment. Behold, I was brought forth in iniquity, and in sin did my mother conceive me. Behold, you delight in truth in the inward being, and you teach me wisdom in the secret heart. Psalm 51:3-6

David is not simply aware of his sin, it has affected him to his core. He is broken. He is destroyed by what he has done. He knows he has sinned against God. There is nothing to redefine or reason away. Sin is to do what is evil according to God. What God says is sin, IS SIN. God defines what is and is not sin. David knows this and owns what he has done as such. This is why David says God is right to judge. Whatever God decides, moving forward is right and just. David understands this is part of his longstanding sinful nature. David is in essence saying, "Sadly this is not an abnormality from an otherwise unblemished life." He understands there has been no time in his life that he has been without sin.

When we understand this, God is the only place to turn. Why? He is the wronged party. Forgiveness and cleansing start with God. We bring Him the life of our sin and He extends forgiveness. Forgiveness involves two parties: the offender and the offended. It consists of the forgiver and the forgiven. David is correctly turning to God.

I got permission from my son to share this. A while back we were playing tennis with other members of our family. He was having an attitude in a way that really gets under my skin. I was trying to correct him, other family members tried as well, but nothing changed. He then did something. I forget what it was, but it caused me to snap. I got in his face screaming. I blew my lid. I embarrassed him. I embarrassed myself. When we got home, he and I talked. I apologized to him privately and then publicly apologized in front of the family. This was just the beginning of a journey though.

This was a journey because I had to honestly admit that this was not a onetime mishap. I often raised my voice at my kids. I had to sit in this. I had to own it. I had to see it. I began to journal and dwell on the depth of my sin in this area. When you take months to look at a shortcoming, you begin seeing it sprout up in many different areas. You get sick of seeing it, at least you ought to. Once I got sick of seeing it- I could then make a change. In that moment, I could not reason away my sin. I was truly wrong. I could not make excuses to lighten my sin, I was truly wrong. I could not point to my upbringing. I was truly wrong. I could not point to my surroundings. I was truly wrong. It was my sin. It was a departure from God's way of doing life and I was wrong.

When we get to the bottom of our bottomless pit of wrong, we find our dead selves. This is the life that Christ came to save. The dead life, the old way of life that can still creep in, is truly a pit of despair. At the bottom of this ugly pit, I see that I have a selfish, self-absorbed, self-centered way of doing life that is utterly contrary to how God would have me live. It is here I fully understand I was absolutely wrong and He is absolutely right. This knowledge is seen in how we move forward. Do we move forward displaying our understanding of our wrong? Humility will mark your pathway forward. Do you move forward knowing He is absolutely right? When you know what better is, you will strive to be better. My son allowed me to share all this because I made him a promise that I would never get in his face like I did that day. If I have not changed I do not deserve to write about it. I know he wouldn't permit me to share this if I haven't changed. He sees Daddy is striving to be better. He and I are stronger through this process.

David continues:

> **Purge me with hyssop, and I shall be clean; wash me, and I shall be whiter than snow. Let me hear joy and gladness; let the bones that you have broken rejoice. Hide your face from my sins, and blot out all my iniquities. Create in me a clean heart, O God, and renew a right spirit within me. Cast me not away from your presence, and take not your Holy Spirit from me. Restore to me the joy of your salvation, and uphold me with a willing spirit.** Psalm 51:7-12

You own your sin and then plunge into your sin -created pit of despair— what a bummer. Yup, but the truth of sin in conjunction with the truth of God knows the deep love of God. Here we begin to understand the depth of God's love for me, that He would even want to take me out of this pit of despair. With the right heart towards God, we do not abuse grace, forgiveness, or God's love. Instead, here is where we own our sin with the great hope found in God's heart for us!

David speaks of crushing bones- sounds painful! His sin and knowledge of his sin have clearly damaged him and his relationship with God. He wants the relationship back, not simply the punishment gone. Confession, what David is doing, does not erase the effects of our wrongs. David's child will still die. Hyssop is symbolic of the removal of sin ceremonially. A restored relationship flows from a cleansing such as this. David here is talking about an act of God, a deep cleansing, where one is no longer seen with the sin. With the barrier of sin removed, a closeness with God can be restored.

Unconfessed sin destroys intimacy. David wants intimacy with God back. He wants the beauty of living in the presence of God's spirit. He wants to know the sustaining power of the Spirit again. He understands his life needs to be renovated and this will only happen by the power of God. David knows the renovation required in his life is a complete transformation; a complete change of life. Here is where David says he needs a "pure heart," a "steadfast spirit" and a "willing spirit." Paul David Tripp says "Sin is a matter of the heart before it is ever an issue of our behavior." Find this and you find a way to move forward transformed!

My 'crushing bones' season was about nine years long. In high school and in college, I messed up sexually before marriage. I hated myself and I hated my sin. I felt unworthy and the unworthy feeling drove me deeper into the sin I hated. The cycle was vicious. I had voices in my life that would remind me of how worthless I was. In that period of life I kept a journal. Can you relate to any of these snippets?

> "Over the last few months, maybe even years,
> I have been feeling worthlessness."

"I have a horrible past, I know I'm forgiven but I don't feel it."

"I'm so stupid, I need to come to grips with what love is. I am a very selfish person. My whole life has been plagued with selfishness, especially in the area of girls. I'm a punk."

"She deserves a pure guy, and that isn't me. I can't change this. It's my past. It hurts. I want to give all of myself to a girl someday, but I can't. I simply can't. When Christ says my sins are washed away, they are forgiven and forgotten- how can that be? How is that possible? My past is a plague. I don't deserve a girl ever."

And that is just the stuff I could put in print, the more appropriate stuff. It is raw and honest. I was hurt and in that place, I felt worthless. I let the worthless feeling be the excuse to drive me to worthless things. The more I drove my life to all that is worthless, I began feeling numb to sin. I was allowing my past sin to become my present sin. I let it damage my walk with Jesus for an extended season of my life.

All leading to perhaps the hardest moment in my journal, writing:

"Hopeless, lost, confused, lonely, depressed, worried, hurt, seeking, searching, wandering: This is life right now. For the first time since I was 13, I have thought about taking my life. It ends all thought. I won't ever truly do that, but as I write, I cry. I am so lost. I want God but I don't know how. I don't have the motivation. I feel so helpless. I want to cry out to God but I feel I don't have a heart anymore. I can spit off head knowledge but do I believe it? I am so lonely and helpless."

What did I need in this place. I needed to be cleansed. I needed to find the real me in Christ Jesus. As you read this, no one is smiling at what is written. This chapter is a sermon delivered in my church. When I read these snippets from my journal, no one applauded. You know who smirked? Know who applauded? Our very real enemy. Satan wants to drive us down to a place of shame. I was there. It is confession that opens the gate for God to drive forward! Confession drives us towards the cleansing we all need!

Cleansing must involve confession. We acknowledge our sin, then we confess it before God. Here, we confess to those we have wronged. We take responsibility and do the necessary things to make it right. People may not accept us back, but this is not about 'being accepted back' or escaping punishment. This is about joining God in restoring what is broken by doing what is right. And when motivated by the gospel, the great love of our Father, we are doing what is right with the right heart!

David continues:

> **Then I will teach transgressors your ways, and sinners will return to you. Deliver me from blood guiltiness, O God, O God of my salvation, and my tongue will sing aloud of your righteousness. O Lord, open my lips, and my mouth will declare your praise. For you will not delight in sacrifice, or I would give it; you will not be pleased with a burnt offering. The sacrifices of God are a broken spirit; a broken and contrite heart, O God, you will not despise. Do good to Zion in your good pleasure; build up the walls of Jerusalem; then will you delight in right sacrifices, in burnt offerings and whole burnt offerings; then bulls will be offered on your altar.** Psalm 51:13-19

True forgiveness is restorative. David is showing what he intends to do moving forward. He is declaring how he will serve God as he rebounds from the pit. The transgressor is now the teacher. The reconciled now bears the message of reconciliation. The more we have experienced God's goodness, the more we ought to tell others about it.

Dear reader, can I get a witness to God's forgiveness? Can someone reading this shout "AMEN" at the thought of being forgiven? Maybe it is because I am writing this chapter and I have just expressed personal aspects of my life, but when I just typed "can I get a witness to God's forgiveness" I smirked. How can forgiveness not bring joy to one's face? Does it for you? Do the people closest to you know your deep failures in the background of God's deep and amazing grace?

"But Jason, come on. Is it that easy for David? Is it that easy for me? David can pen a few words that we now call Psalm 51 and move forward." It is anything but easy. True confession and actual ownership are hard. It should be hard. My sin cost the life of the Son! Sin is rectified through confession and repentance. This is where we need to understand that old fuddy-duddy word "contrite" or "contrition." Type on "define contrite" on Google and Google spits back; "feeling or expressing remorse or penitence; affect by guilt."

Without a broken and contrite heart on the part of the offender, God finds no pleasure in sacrifice and burnt offerings. Good deeds must accompany good promises. It is owning your wrong, committing to better, and then living it out! The sincerity of David's confession, like ours, will be demonstrated by obedient service. Forgiveness is, in a sense, the removal of evil. However, to be restorative, the exercising of good must follow. This is seen in the closing verses of the Psalm we just read.

Ava and I had a moment a few weeks back where we did our family devotions, sent kids to bed. After they went to bed, some of the stuff from the day left us sitting numbly on the couch. We went to bed broken because we were confronted with the fact that we cannot shelter our kids from the filth and horrors of this world. My kids are growing up and this is a reality. We each woke up with the desire to put our kids in a bubble. Have you been there for your loved ones?

Think about this. I have kids. You are someone's kid. I am someone's kid. My wife, parents, and even my grandparents heard this preached as a sermon. I hope someday my kids will read this book. Ok, great. But think about how I have opened up. You can read between the lines and know my deep sin. My parents could not shelter me, they could not protect me. They tried as all good parents do, but at some point, humans are humans. But what my parents could do, and did do, was introduce me to the Great Forgiver and Great Restorer. You see, all people fail, but few know the amazing grace of my Jesus. I cannot shelter my kids, but may they know their deep wrongs in the backdrop of His amazing grace. May they understand their sins in the ocean of His mercy. It was what was taught to me and what I hope to pass on to my kids.

My thoughts become the enemy's playground when I battle with sin. My kids will fight with their thinking as well. This Psalm combats all that Satan would have us feel and think in the midst of our sins.

"I am useless" vs. "No, I will teach your people:"

"I can't be forgiven" vs. "Cleanse me!"

"I will earn my way back to His good graces" vs.
"I offer my broken and contrite heart"

"I suck" vs. "Lord, restore the joy of your salvation"

In sin, may we all remember the joy of our salvation. May we remember the Lord wants all of us. He wants our sin, our brokenness, our heart, all of us. He wants me. He wants you. If we were to boil this down to one point to walk away with it would be this; **God's heart loves a contrite heart.** The pathway to experience the joy of your salvation is remembering God's heart for you while you bring Him your contrite heart.

What made David die "successful" in God's eyes was not perfection but contrition. He knew his sin, he let himself feel brokenness and went to God in that brokenness for restoration. The person of faith experiences success as we bring our struggles, weaknesses, and battles with sin to the stronger One! It is God's grace that He wants to help us out and make us better.

I have seen my earthly dad broken as I am broken. But, I have learned many great things from him. He played college tennis, as did I. I learned the right teams to cheer for. You know, all the important stuff! My dad, like his son, is flawed. As I have a flawed dad, my boys have a flawed dad. But honestly, the greatest lesson I have learned from him is "own your wrong." He would tell me not to beat around the bush, own it. I learned from him to "own my 1%." Meaning, even if I am only 1% in the wrong, you own it. If you have fault, own your fault. Do not worry about the other 99%, it is not yours to own. Just worry about what is yours to own and own it!

The truly contrite own their 1%. The truly contrite are not worried or focused on the 99% remaining. The truly contrite will own their part no matter how big or small. Contrition requires confession. Is there a wrong you need to own through confession? Is there something you have needed to confess but you have seen as "not a big deal" in light of everything else in the situation?

Here are three types of confession to consider:

Confession of Faith: At the beginning of Chapter 7 we shared what it means to give your heart to Jesus. You and I have sinned. You and I share hearts that wander from the perfection God desires and demands. The confession of faith is declaring to God you accept the gift His Son has offered to us. You declare, without excuse or justification, that you have sinned and are wrong. He is right and just to see me as a sinner that deserves a sinner's penalty. You declare gratitude and acceptance of what was accomplished through Jesus Christ by dying on the cross and then raising three days later to extend to us life. This is where a life of confession starts. Have you accepted Jesus Christ as your personal Savior? It is time for a personal confession of faith between you and Jesus.

> **But what does it say? "The word is near you, in your mouth and in your heart" (that is, the word of faith that we proclaim); 9 because, if you confess with your mouth that Jesus is Lord and believe in your heart that God raised him from the dead, you will be saved. 10 For with the heart one believes and is justified, and with the mouth, one confesses and is saved. 11 For the Scripture says, "Everyone who believes in him will not be put to shame."** Romans 10:8-11

Confession of Sin to man: This is where we own our wrong to whom we have wronged. Did you overspend on your household budget? You owe your family an apology, along with your plan to do better. Did you steal food from the lunch line? Apologize and pay for it. Did you cheat on your spouse? Confess it. It is simply not possible to move forward in complete restoration without this step. We said that restoration involves two people: the wronged and the one in the wrong. Confession owns your wrong while inviting the other person into the process. In the healthy Christian community, we should find people owning their wrongs with contrition. Those people should be met with those willing to forgive as they have been forgiven. Then together, we all move forward, becoming more like Jesus Christ. Whom have you wronged? Go, confess now. Make it right.

> **Whoever conceals his transgressions will not prosper, but he who confesses and forsakes them will obtain mercy.** Proverbs 28:13

Confession of Sin to the Son of Man: God, through Jesus Christ has forgiven me of my sin! Yup, that is the confession of sin we mentioned first.

Before God, we are seen as perfect because we have the perfection of Christ. Yet, daily we still fail to live perfectly. We need to own this. The confession of faith brings our overall life of sin and places it before Jesus. As we move forward, we continue to bring our everyday sins to Him. Although we committed to walk and become more like Jesus on a daily basis, here is where we confess to God when this has not taken place. We have wronged the very one who sent His Son to die for us—all while being a person who understands the truth. Where, in prayer, do you need to confess sin to God? How did you wrong Him? Your fellow man? What thoughts are far from Him? Bring all your sins to Him! He has been gracious and He will continue to be gracious as you come to Him in contrition.

> **If we say we have no sin, we deceive ourselves, and the truth is not in us. 9 If we confess our sins, he is faithful and just to forgive us our sins and to cleanse us from all unrighteousness. 10 If we say we have not sinned, we make him a liar, and his word is not in us.** 1 John 1:8-10

Our hearts will fail. We will wander from God. But, there is a pathway forward. Take it. Cling to the heart of Jesus. When we take hold of Christ's heart, we begin to walk in His ways. This is the way to a successful life!

PART TWO

THE RESULTS

RESULT #1: FAVOR
BIBLICAL CASE STUDY

Let not steadfast love and faithfulness forsake you;
bind them around your neck; write them on
the tablet of your heart. So you will find favor…"

"Grace is the overflowing favor of God, and you can
always count on it being available to draw upon
as needed." **Oswald Chambers**

*B*iblical success is when God's heart and God's ways become my heart and my way. As we live this out, what can we expect? As we put all the ingredients into the mixer, what do we expect to eventually come out of the oven? In our verse, God gives us three results; favor, success with God, and success with man. We will tackle a biblical case study for each of these results and conclude with a chapter to summarize. Our first biblical case study starts with a man who had the favor of God, leading to the building of a boat-Noah.

As I turned the page from 2021 to 2022, I decided it was time to kick it into gear. I set my goals and instantly started attacking life. Beachbody has a program called Insanity. It is a workout program you can do at home but given the title, it is insane and intense—halfway through they give you a 'recovery' week with lighter workouts. So, I hit the gym one day to do the elliptical. The elliptical is my typical workout but I had not done it for over a month. As soon as I started my workout, I realized that through insanity my cardio had improved. I crushed my workout. With ten minutes left I put on my workout playlist and pushed myself to the brink of exhaustion. I got done and was gassed. I felt literal pain. So like the good millennial I am, I went on social media and posted "pain is my reward." To this, I received responses from people letting me know they were praying for me! I guess people needed a little context! My point, with the context, was that I felt pain and the pain I felt was the result of a great workout. My pain was positive because I had done something positive. Pain, given the nature of what I was trying to accomplish, was part of the reward. It is what I should expect when I have an incredible workout.

Faulty expectations lead to disillusionment. If you think a workout should not leave you feeling pain or exhaustion, you will quit early. Favor is much like this. We have faulty expectations. We think if we do X, God will do Y. But is God's favor really a math equation? Is it really tit for tat? That sounds more like religion than a relationship. Give enough and I'll get enough. Read enough and God will do this for me. Pray enough and I'll get the job.

God's favor *may* include promotions, financial gain, family, health, etc. It may consist of these things, but it is rarer than we think. These things, what we typically see as favor, are definitely not the end all be all. They are never to be the focus. God is the focus. A conversation on favor that takes the focus off the Father is a misguided conversation. Does God show favor just to show favor? Does He show favor with a purpose? What is the purpose? This is where we put the focus on God and ask Him to define favor. This is where we look to the Father to understand *why* He bestows favor to His children.

If what God sees as favor is different from what we see as favor, then when God shows us His favor, we will not feel His favor. Why? Our expectations and understanding is different than the One who bestows the gift. Maybe it is God's favor that you do not get the promotion. Maybe it is God's favor that you don't have a new car in the driveway because it would change your character. Could it be the enemy brings to our lives some of the "nice things" we typically see as favor only to move us away from God? Perhaps the enemy himself is playing right into our faulty view of favor to distract us from the very one who bestows true favor on His children!

Let's use our time to look at a man who is said to have had the favor of God. Noah is truly and legitimately, the last faithful person on earth. He is "like legit" one in a million. What would you expect favor to look like? A new car? Big bank account? Big house? Oh, favor for Noah plays out so differently!

At the start of Genesis 6, what is mentioned is theologically debated. The text mentions angels sleeping with humans. And you thought the Bible was boring! This is one of the most confusing passages in all of Scripture. For the scope and purpose of what we are doing here, we will not enter into the debate. Those more educated than I am point to these angels as descendants of Seth and/or Cain. These could indeed be angels. They could be people from the line of David. They could be rulers. Here is the point, something very sinful is happening on earth. What is said, although confusing to the modern reader, is proof of the depravity of mankind.

How terrible has man's depravity become? They are abusing marriage. They are taking who they want when they want. They have perverted the world to a state of injustice. What started with Eden, now has become a world filled with violence. They are people assuming themselves to be deities.

Their actions are literally breeding results. The population is exploding. Those being born of these sinful actions are mighty and attractive. More and 'better' people you would think is a sign of God's favor. Nope! Humanity was growing but as is often the case, growth in worldly ways often leads to spiritual decay; more rarely makes us better. They were careless sexually. They were careless with marriage. They were simply careless. Yes, they had results. Yes, they would look at the results and *feel* successful. Success in worldly ways made them careless, corrupt, complacent, and willing to compromise. Here we are thousands of years later and human nature is unchanged.

Did God see them as successful? No, not at all! So He says, in essence, "y'all got 120 years." This is God's response to what He sees:

5 The Lord saw that the wickedness of man was great in the earth, and that every intention of the thoughts of his heart was only evil continually. 6 And the Lord regretted that he had made man on the earth, and it grieved him to his heart. 7 So the Lord said, "I will blot out man whom I have created from the face of the land, man and animals and creeping things and birds of the heavens, for I am sorry that I have made them." Genesis 6:5-7

Did the wicked mentioned in this passage appear to be prosperous by the standards of the world? What God saw as wicked, did the world see itself as successful? This is a sad truth still present today as I type; God sees much of what we say is good and right as wicked. What God sees, He regrets. This is a complicated word. There are ten different words for this one Hebrew word. One commentary says, "I propose this word can be best understood in accounting terms. In bookkeeping, the ledgers must always be kept in balance; debits equals credits. If the books get out of balance, something must be adjusted." In other words, God looked at humanity with this notion that you have been weighed and found wanting.

We have this in our society as well. I want to be the pastor who speaks into culture not against culture. It is subtle but protects me from being all doom and gloom. With that, as I read about the days of Noah, I do not see much has changed in our day. God is disappointed. We must not pretend that we have arrived or that God should look upon our generation with great joy in what we have become.

Think about this as a God-fearing Christian: God's heart can grieve. Our actions bring His heart grief. God does not respond with a fit of anger. God is not throwing a temper tantrum. There are no thunderbolts. No, in fact, grief is a word indicative of love. We do not grieve those we do not love. Many people die each day, but I only grieve the loss of some. The word "grieved" here shows God's care and desire for these people. In His grieved heart, God makes the decision to destroy and restart. As a divine Creator, this is His divine right.

My personal restart prompted this book. A good restart, humanly speaking, takes what has been awful and makes it better. In 2021, a word I focused on for the year was "stabilize." We survived the chaos of 2020, praise God. In

2021, I felt I needed to focus on stabilizing all aspects of my life: church, family, etc. 2021 was successful in that framework. The church was stable and moving ahead. My family found new normal and routines. For me, this led to what felt like average and boring. In my personal life, I was flabby. I gained weight. My time with Jesus was present but stale. My eating was ok. My workouts were bland. Church and family stabilized. However, although I was stable, I was not necessarily healthy. For my personality, I am healthiest when I am in attack mode without losing sight of grace toward the people I serve. I lost that. So at the turn of the year, I focused on the word "attack." Here is where we launched Pizza Church, as previously mentioned. In 2022 I set up six goals to help me attack the year:

1. Fun: Hike a 14,000-foot mountain.

2. Faith: Finish writing a book.

3. Fitness: Get to a healthy BMI.

4. Financial: Save a three month emergency fund.

5. Family: Initiate a year of discipleship for my son Landon.

6. Friends: Take a family vacation with another family.

I looked at my life and knew I needed to make a shift. These goals have me hyper-focused on change. If you are reading this, you are reading a result of this restart. Sometimes a good restart is needed. Before we go any further in our discussion on favor, where does your life need a good restart? Where does your life need a jump start?

What is needed for a good restart? A deep burning discontent for the current reality. A deep understanding of why this current reality is not good. An understanding of what a better reality looks like. An articulated plan to get there. Here is where we can take a Dwight Schutt 'ism' and say, "I ask myself what an idiot would do, and then I do not do that thing." A restart is the opposite. I am the idiot (said lightly), so I ask myself, what would someone crushing it do in an area I am lacking, then I do that thing. What would it look like to be the best Christian employee at work? Go do that thing. What would it look like to be the best Christian student in your school? Go do that thing. What would it look like to be the best Christian child in my family? Go do that thing. What would it look like to be the best Christian parent in my family? Go do that thing. What would it look like to be the best Christian in my church family? Go do that thing. Many of us need a good restart. Let's get at it!

Our text continues;

> **But Noah found favor in the eyes of the Lord. These are the generations of Noah. Noah was a righteous man, blameless in his generation. Noah walked with God.** Genesis. 6:8-9

When I think of my life those last four words rock me. I hope when it all comes to an end that it will be said of me, "Jason walked with God." It was said of Noah. As God looked over the earth, literally one person found favor with God. Noah is not a minor biblical character. He is referenced over fifty times in eleven different books of the Bible. Why? Noah walked with God. Why? He was faithful. Why? He was seen as just.

Noah's righteousness did not come from his good works. His good works came because of his righteousness. Noah was righteous and so did good things. This is why he is described as blameless. If 'righteous' describes Noah's standing before God, then 'blameless' describes his conduct before people. Blameless does not mean sinless, it means you have integrity and are largely unblemished. The person who is right before God through faith in Christ ought to lead a life that is right before people. Noah walked with God and justly before people.

Live and be the only one left on earth being faithful to God. God found this favorable and extended favor. However, catch this, it is critical. If you are Noah, the last faithful person on earth, what would you expect God's favor to look like? With an understanding of favor as God defines favor, here is the better question; what would God's favor cost Noah?

God's favor led to work. God granted Noah favor and this favor led to Noah's assignment. Obedience and favor go hand in hand. Favor is more like a promotion than it is a bonus. Yet, we treat it like a bonus; extra PTO days, a new car, fat check, etc. When really it resembles more of the promotion structure. You have been a faithful employee, let me give you more responsibilities. The promotion comes with greater work. Obedience for Noah led to favor and favor furthered obedience. Noah was given a 120-year building project. He was assigned the building of an ark. This was his reward.

Earlier I mentioned my goals for the year. One of my goals is to establish a year of discipleship with my son, Landon. It is a concept Mark Batterson talks about in his book *Play the Man*. Landon is turning 12. He is about to enter what many consider to be manhood. I am going to take a year and hyper-focus on him for this "year of discipleship." So to use our terms, during this year, I will favor my son Landon. I will invest around $2,000 into him when it's all said and done. I will invest countless hours and a monthly lunch with him. What will this favor cost him? He will have to read 12 books. He will have to read through the New Testament. He will have to hike about forty miles in four days eagle scout style. He has to plan an outreach with the people in charge of outreach for our church (plan and execute). He will get certified as a "wilderness first responder." Then to end our time, we will have one last epic hike with a 'graduation' moment at the end of it. My favor for him is to prepare him and focus on him. I will favor him because he is my son. I am not doing this for your son. Just mine. My favor is based on relationship, position, and proximity.

Did Noah know this building project would work out? No. But the faithful remained faithful. Will Landon fully get what my efforts aligned with his efforts are all about? No. Will he complain? Yes. Will he be better for it? Yes. Will he look back on our time together as a highlight of his childhood? I sure hope so. Noah, the real example here, simply continued doing what was asked of him even when it was costly and foolish looking.

Faith is doing what we do not fully understand. Faith takes a step when we cannot see where our foot will land. Faith will require us to build a boat in a desert because rain and floods are coming to a people that have never seen anything like that before. Favor looks foolish. Noah looked foolish. Sarah looked ridiculous buying maternity clothes at 99. David looked foolish attacking Goliath with a slingshot. Moses looked foolish asking Pharaoh to let his slaves go. The Israelite army looked silly marching around Jericho blowing trumpets. BUT RESULTS SPEAK FOR THEMSELVES.

Perhaps we need to focus on looking a little more foolish. Perhaps if you are not willing to look a little foolish you are the foolish one.[2] Protect yourself from ever looking foolish in the world's eyes? God sees this as foolish. To the world, the faithful walk looks like a foolish walk. But, if you protect yourself from looking foolish you will never build an ark, kill a giant or walk on water like Peter, if only for a moment.

Here is what I hope we see through our time with Noah thinking about favor: *when God 'floats your boat,' He may ask you to build a boat!*

Favor opens up opportunities, but will we see them as opportunities? Will God's favor feel like "a great opportunity" as we are faithfully grinding for our King? Will we seize the opportunity afforded to us by God's favor? Will we embrace the hardship and pain God's favor brings our way?

Mary was favored, was she not? The angel said "o favored one." (Luke 1:28). What did God's favor lead to? Pain; Living with the reputation, in a very religious culture, of being sexually disobedient. How did that religious culture treat people with a sinful reputation? Terribly. She likely lost her husband Joseph during Jesus' childhood. What would it have been like to be widowed with a sexually sinful reputation in Israel during biblical times? Terrible. She was there to see her son die a brutal death on a cross. Can you imagine? But she was favored. She, unlike any other mother on earth, helped raise a truly perfect son. She found God's favor and lived a faithful life to the end.

Mark Batterson in his book *All In* speaks of Noah and Jewish traditions that are shocking. According to Batterson, did you know Noah had to start by planting trees that when fully grown, he would cut down and use to build the ark? Noah had to get creative to get the job done. He had to patiently wait for his resources to literally grow up out of the ground. This is long obedience. As Batterson points out, from start to finish, Noah's act of obedience would take about 43,800 days. That is some assignment for being the last faithful person on earth!

We think we live a very dedicated life before God. What is a fair ask of God? When do we start looking to God saying, "enough?" Moses was faithful for

---

[2] Concepts from Mark Batterson's *All In*.

40 plus years. Joseph was in jail for years and years. He was a slave for years and years. Noah had a 120-year assignment. Yet we want to punk out thinking we have lived a dedicated life when we have given God a month or two for a given challenge. Will God's favor propel you to be faithful for decades? God wants our lives not just our "insta" moments.

Life on the ark would not have been a cake walk, as they say. Thousands of pounds of poop would have had to have been shoveled out each day. Obedience is hard work and gets harder as the days go on. That is God's favor and blessing for you. It will complicate your life. However, unlike sin, it will complicate your life in a way it should be complicated. Choose your complication. I have a healthy and solid marriage. It is daily work and it is hard work. I can sin and exit my marriage. Either way, life is complicated, but I have chosen a better complication. I can live as if gluttony is not a sin and that will add complications to my life. Or I can live as if 2,000 calories is a healthy amount of calories to eat each day, tracking every bite. It is constant work and gets complicated at dinner time. I have chosen a better complication that leads to a healthier life. You will choose how to complicate your life. Choose Jesus.

Are you willing to be the last faithful Christian on earth? Are you willing, truly, to be the last one to worship the One true God? To stand absolutely alone in love for God almighty? If the answer, with conviction, is yes, then we talk about favor. What does day in and day out obedience look like for you in light of God's favor in your life? Is God favored in your finances? Is God favored in your schedule? Is God favored in your God-given abilities? Think deeply on this. In light of how you have answered these questions, what changes do you need to make? Does worship for the King motivate these changes? Are there areas you feel God's blessing and favor? What act of obedience is God calling you into in light of that favor?

Let me tell you about my neighbor Todd. When I met Todd he was working as a supervisor at Comcast. His shift had him working weekends and late into the evening. As we talked, he would tell me that when he retired, he would start coming to my church. If I am honest, I thought he was full of poo poo and playing me with nice sentiments. Todd, a super kind guy, was kind of forced out of his job because he would not play some of the corporate games of management. Todd retired early. First Sunday after he retired, he came to Wellspring. I think I could count on one hand how many Sundays he's missed since that day a few years ago. Todd is now leading a recovery life group for my church. He attends my men's group. He has helped us launch Pizza Church in our hometown. I am privileged to walk through premarital counseling with him and his fiancé. Todd noticed he was blessed with free time and you know how he decided to fill his time? He serves the local homeless ministry. His main job is that when the weather dips into the 30's or below, he travels to tent communities around our county and invites them to the shelter, giving them a ride.

Todd had God's favor through an early retirement and a favorable severance package. There was no super long and exclusive vacation. Todd began serving others. He has come alive. When you talk to him, he speaks of how blessed his life is. He is blessed to serve others. Favor propelled service.

If you started reading this chapter expecting a prosperity talk like you will find on TV, you now have unmet expectations. I hope this has been a new understanding of favor. With this new understanding, where might God be showing you favor, creating an opportunity to serve the King? What will you do about it?

RESULT #2: SUCCESS WITH GOD
BIBLICAL CASE STUDY

Let not steadfast love and faithfulness forsake you;
bind them around your neck; write them on the tablet
of your heart. So you will find favor and good
success in the sight of God…"

"Our greatest fear should not be of failure but of succeeding
at things in life that don't really matter." **Francis Chan**

*B*iblical success is when God's heart and God's ways become my heart and my way. As we live this out, what can we expect? Having spent time examining the favor of God, we now focus on success with God. How does one live a successful life? Live a life the King sees as successful!

Growing up I drank roughly 2 liters of soda each day. In fact, my biggest fight ever with my wife was over soda. What should have been laughable then is laughable now. Yup a fight over soda. Nowadays, I have the occasional coke zero but by and large it is out of my life. Whenever I would cut soda out of my diet, I quickly lost ten pounds. In one of my many weight loss attempts, it really hit me how cutting soda out of my diet had a positive impact on my body. So I did a little research. Did you know it takes about four days for soda to completely dissolve a nail. A metal nail! Completely dissolved. Now imagine what it is doing to your body! I know this. So here is my question: foolish or wise for me to continue drinking soda?

If you understand a truth, wisdom or foolishness is on full display in your response. How you respond to stated truth will define you as a fool or wise person. The way you respond to truth produces results. The Bible is full of this talk, just read the Sermon on the Mount in Matthew 5-7 or the entire book of James to start! Fruit is telling. When I understood the truth of soda and made a change, I had the fruit of losing ten quick pounds. When I ignored the truth of soda, I had the fruit of keeping those ten pounds on.

What fruit is being produced based on your understanding of the King? If God has invested His Spirit into you, you have God-given talents. You have God-given talent through the Spirit empowering you to be a kingdom builder! If God has invested in the person of the Holy Spirit and has given you a spiritual gift, is it not fair for Him to expect a return on investment? Jesus tells a story along these lines:

> **14 "For it will be like a man going on a journey, who called his servants and entrusted to them his property. 15 To one he gave five talents, to another two, to another one, to each according to his ability. Then he went away. 16 He who had received the five talents went at once and traded with them, and he made five talents more. 17 So also he who had the two talents made two talents more. 18 But he who had received the one talent went and dug in the ground and hid his master's money.** Matthew 25:14-18

The keyword in this passage is *entrusted*. The key concept is *according to ability*. The master examined the servant, knew the servant, thought through what they could handle and charged them with money accordingly. The one-talent dude still got a lot of money. One commentary I read said it could be as much as $247,200 in today's terms. Either way, to varying degrees, all three servants have been entrusted with a large sum of money. The master entrusted what is His to someone who does not initially have ownership. It is temporary ownership.

All of a sudden, the master leaves. These three servants have more money in their physical possession than they have ever presumably had! Two of them immediately use the money, take an insane amount of risk, trade the money and *double* the money. Those risky frisky servants experienced a great payoff for their actions! They used what they had and gained more. Success!

The third? He did almost nothing. Took care not to lose it but did nothing positive with the masters' money to create gains; played it safe by digging and hiding it. If I am honest, does this not seem logical? If we didn't know the pay off, on paper this seems logical. Would we not be praising this guy if the other two had lost it all? In this regard, the actions of the third is the *natural* action many of us would take.

Two of them hustled. One of them sat on his hands. Two of them lived into their potential and one of them wasted his potential. This may be natural for us, but natural is all too common in today's church. Too many of us are sitting on our hands wasting our legit God-given talent and potential.

I grew up in New England, as I have mentioned numerous times. I am a proud New Englander and lover of all things Boston sports. Was I hurt when Tom Brady left the Patriots and joined the Tampa Bay Bucs? Sure, but I get it. Old people always head south. Then Rob Gronkowski (D.B.A. Gronk - ha!) came out of retirement, worked a trade and signed with the Bucs. The glory days of the Patriots are now in Tampa! So, all that to say, I still follow these two individuals. One article that recently came across my newsfeed was about how Gronk took advantage of COVID for his off-season workouts. All the players had daily workouts they needed to do, but with COVID, they had to stay home. So the coaching staff made them take videos of the workouts and send them in to hold them accountable to do them. Gronk? The freak athlete and party animal that he is decided that he would work hard for one day and then coast the rest of the off-season. How? He did all his workouts one day, changing his shirt each time and then sent the coaching staff a clip each day. Genius. If the coaching staff was present, Gronk never would have acted like this. In the coaching staff's absence, Gronk did something funny to us but not funny to them. They would see this as a waste of potential.

The talent being talked about in this passage was not a coin, rather it is seen as a measure of weight—a talent of gold or a talent of silver. Worth of the talent was determined by the type of coin it was. So there is an appropriate application to apply this to the talents of our lives. What resources have we been given as seen in our time, finances, abilities, and power? Not everyone is born with the same talents, and not everyone is endowed with the same gifts of the Spirit. Yet each one of us can be productive in our own unique ways for the kingdom. The talent being weighed may be different, but we all have talent being weighed!

> **19 Now after a long time the master of those servants came and settled accounts with them. 20 And he who had received the five talents came forward, bringing five talents more, saying, 'Master, you delivered to me five talents; here, I have made five talents more.' 21 His master said to him, 'Well done, good and faithful servant. You have been faithful over a little; I will set you over much. Enter into the joy of your master.' 22 And he also who had the two talents came forward, saying, 'Master, you delivered to me two talents; here, I have made two talents more.' 23 His master said to him, 'Well done, good and faithful servant. You have been faithful over a little; I will set you over much. Enter into the joy of your master.'** Matthew 25:19-23

Although the master waits an undisclosed amount of time, the servants felt like it was a long time. Upon return, everything is exposed. There is no hiding. Accountability was built into what was originally entrusted. With all exposed, the two-talent guy and the five-talent guy hear the same thing from the master: WELL DONE, GOOD AND FAITHFUL SERVANT! They both took risks and both doubled the money. They took a risk in line with the master's heart. Just because the one doubled more money did not mean he heard something different. Why? This was about taking risks in line with the heart of the master. It was the action, not the amount that was rewarded. It shows the master looked for goodness and faithfulness and saw their actions as such. Their success was due to their good and faithful actions. The focus, again catch this, was not the money, it was proof of the character behind what they had done. So, yes, come and enjoy the joy of the Lord! Spurgeon said, "this is not the servant's portion, but the Master's portion shared with His faithful servants… not so much that we shall have a joy of our own as that we shall enter into the joy of our Lord." The Lord is sharing His subsequent joy with those who have helped create the joy.

Recently, my family and I went on vacation to Orlando, Florida. My boys were finally at the height where they could go on the "big boy" rides. One day we went to the Island of Adventure. We watched YouTube videos on the park and the rides. People travel from all over the world to hit some of these rides. One ride in particular people specifically come to experience is VelociCoaster. This ride has its own Wikipedia page! It will take you 155 feet in the air at a speed of 70 miles per hour. It is an insane ride.

So, when we got to the park, my boys and I rushed over to ride it. It was a decent wait, but we did it. While in line I was talking it up and trying to scare them, because I'm Dad of the year ha! They were brave. My 9- and 11-year-old kids did it and loved it. Later in the day they wanted to do it again. So, in an effort to give them an appropriate amount of freedom (guiding growing freedom), I let them do the ride on their own. I walked them to the entrance, told them to stick together and before putting cell phones in lockers to text me. I would meet them at the end of the ride. They got to the security checkpoint right before getting on the ride where you have to place your cell phones in a locker and there was no cell service. After waiting two hours, they got out of line. TWO HOURS. Why? Because they could not completely follow the rules to the letter of the law. I was like, WHAT, BOYS!!! COME ON. I'd see the text go through when you get cell service. I'd understand, get on the ride!

They did not fully understand my heart. They are in the process of learning how I want them to handle life when I am not around. I am in the process of teaching them my heart. We have mutual responsibilities as learner and teacher. As this process goes on, there are times I leave them at home now. When I return? You bet your bottom dollar there is accountability! I am looking to see if they handled themselves the way I would have wanted them to handle themselves. Sometimes I give them a heads up that I am five minutes away so they can be ready with the house cleaned and pretend like they still like each other. Other times, I just show up so I can catch them with the element of surprise. They "look" better when I give them the heads up. When I surprise them, it is often messier but I get a better snapshot of the real them. Sometimes it is super positive, other times it gives us things to talk about.

What does it look like to be ready for our Master to return? Are you prepared for the King to return? What is He looking for? What does this communicate about the heart of our King? As you read the passage, multiplication is what He is looking for. Are you building the King's kingdom? Are you taking risks to be a kingdom builder? Being a kingdom builder will not look "safe" in the moment. But two servants are "safe" when the master returns because they were risky in multiplication while the king was away! Who are you praying to come to faith and how are you willing to be used by God for this to happen? Are you willing to get risky to see others come to faith? If the King returns and asks "how many more people are in the Kingdom because of you?" What would you say? What is reality? Will He find you getting risky or sitting on your hands?

We have to be kingdom builders in all areas of our lives. We have to use the social media, the coffee shop, our time at work, sidelines of our kids sports, the geometry group project, our mom's group. Whatever natural means we have, we must use to build God's kingdom! Whatever means possible to reach as many people as possible as quickly as possible! Are you ready to give account for your kingdom efforts? Have you been productive in the King's "absence?" If yes, come enter into the joy that is yours! The joy of being on mission with the King is an eternally shared joy. Sitting on your hands, that is the joyless life!

24 He also who had received the one talent came forward, saying, 'Master, I knew you to be a hard man, reaping where you did not sow, and gathering where you scattered no seed, 25 so I was afraid, and I went and hid your talent in the ground. Here, you have what is yours.' 26 But his master answered him, 'You wicked and slothful servant! You knew that I reap where I have not sown and gather where I scattered no seed? 27 Then you ought to have invested my

money with the bankers, and at my coming I should have received what was my own with interest. Matthew 25:24-27

The master judged them individually. The one-talent servant has to account for why he did what he did. Why did he act this way? A poor view of the master! Our inaccurate views of God become our rationalization for our own sinfulness. We see this on full display here. Had this servant truly loved the master, he would not have attempted to place blame on the master for being a hard man. He knows the master produces results. He knew the master was big and mighty. His attitude is such that he could not live up to the master, so this is why he did not even try. What he thought of the master overpowered any desire he had to please the master. If he had good FOMO (fear of missing out), he would have feared missing out on hearing "well done, good and faithful servant." He would have invested instead of buried.

What do the results of our lives speak to? No kingdom work? No habit of prayer? No evangelistic efforts? Is this not spiritual laziness? One day God will respond to the spiritually lazy. We rarely see laziness as a major sin, but God takes it very seriously. We view righteousness usually by the good we have done or the wrong we have not done. We view a lack of righteousness by, catch this, simply the wrong we have done. We rarely see a lack of righteousness in people who could have done good and chose not to. But that is just as much a part of righteousness as anything else. The master looks and says, "Come on! You could have at least invested with bankers to gain some interest, but you did not! You did nothing. You could have done something even if it did not double. BUT YOU DID NOTHING." He is held responsible for the nothing (good) he chose to do. How seriously did the master take this omission? The servant not only did not hear those "well done" words, as if that were bad enough, he was also declared wicked for laziness. His failure to act and his laziness got him the title of wicked.

I have referenced my college and post-college portion of my life a few times in this book. It is a dark time in my life. I was lazy in so many ways. I was butthurt and mad at God because I had to transfer schools for financial reasons. I was mad that my pastor was forced out of the church back home. Mad led to excuses, and excuses led to sin. I was angry, but in my anger, I went to sin instead of going to God. So here I am working at American Eagle, at the Oxford Valley Mall by my college. I went to a Bible school, and by association with my college I was known at work as a Christian. I was the only Christian most of them knew. I was their reference point to Christianity. What did I do with that opportunity? I partied. I hit up the clubs. I was involved with girls. I had a moment by the front table of American Eagle folding polos with some other associates, where we were talking about hitting the bars after work, when one of them stopped and said, "aren't you a Christian? Can you do this?" My response was perhaps the only honest thing I said in months, "I am, but I am not living it. You can't look at my life and see Jesus." I went on to encourage him not to judge Jesus by my actions. Cool, way to go Jason. So did that change you? Nope, I went on partying. A moment of truth but a life left unchanged. How many opportunities did I squander by sitting on my evangelistic hands? Will there be people in hell because I sat on my hands? Yes, God is big. Yes, salvation rests on God. Yes, yes, yes, I know this. Yet, it is still a question I ask myself because it is an honest question based on how I lived in those moments. I will be held accountable not only for what I did in that time of my life, but also for what I did not do. I will be held accountable for my spiritual laziness.

My attitude then, along with the wicked servant, is precisely how many today deal with God. They have the wrong thoughts, feelings or attitude towards God, leading to excuses for disobedience. We see God as mean or unconcerned, so we live against the will of God. They see God as unloving, so they do not join Him on mission, loving the world around them. Truth is God is crazy about you and crazy about reaching others through you! God has gifted you to build His kingdom. We call that a spiritual gift. Every child of God has one. It is time to think more highly of the God who is crazy about you and get on mission for Him. Stop sitting on your spiritually lazy hands and start putting that gift to use for Kingdom purposes.

28 So take the talent from him and give it to him who has the ten talents. 29 For to everyone who has will more be given, and he will have an abundance. But from the one who has not, even what he has will be taken away. 30 And cast the worthless servant into the outer darkness. In that place there will be weeping and gnashing of teeth. Matthew 25:28-30

Did the third servant anticipate the master's pleasure while the master was gone? Did he anticipate that the master would return and be proud of him? I think many are walking this earth right now anticipating God will be proud of them when they meet Him. Do they woefully misunderstand the situation like this third servant? How many feel eternally safe yet are not? Jesus does not grade on a curve and there are no retakes.

This third servant, no matter how he expected the situation to play out, is cast into outer darkness. He does not gain. He loses. He did not share the master's heart so he is cast away from the master forever. Not a time, forever! But those who did share the master's heart? They are entrusted with more. What was initially given to the wicked servant is given to the faithful servants. Meaning, what is entrusted to me, if mishandled, can be entrusted to another.

As this wicked servant is cast away, as if that is not bad enough, how is he described? Worthless. Let that sink in. If you have a personality like mine, this word hits you at your core. I do not want to be seen as worthless. I do not want to spend time on worthless things. I do not want to lose everything. I want my life to count and to matter. The trustworthy stand to gain. The worthless- those who cannot be trusted- will lose. There are two eternal destinations. We will each arrive at one of these two destinations. What destination currently awaits you? Have you given your life to Jesus? No? Consider long and hard what awaits you. Will you one day arrive in heaven as your destination? It is time to start living like it.

My wife is self-employed. She owns her own business as a real estate appraiser. Unlike many in our nation, her taxes are not automatically taken out of each paycheck. As Ava was being trained and learning the industry she had good and bad examples on how to handle taxes. Any spreadsheet lovers? Well, I am in that club. Having learned the dangers of not being prepared, I created a spreadsheet. Ava gives me her weekly pay; I put that number into a spreadsheet. The spreadsheet auto generates, taking 25% out for taxes and giving me a number to put into our monthly budget. As the year goes on, our bank account has thousands of dollars in it. But does it? It may look like we have tons of money, but it is all for taxes. The key is simply not spending it!

Yearly, there is a moment of truth. We sit down with our tax guy and he says "how much have you put away for taxes?" I then share the spreadsheet. Every year he says he wishes he had our discipline because he should save throughout the year like we do. Instead, he works all of tax season just to pay his taxes. That moment when he asks me if we saved for taxes is never stressful. I am prepared for that moment. I knew it was coming and acted accordingly. We never get to January and think, "oh crap, we should start saving for taxes."

These servants had a moment of truth coming. They were responsible for what was entrusted to them. Where Ava and I have a weekly habit to prepare us for a future financial reckoning, our evangelistic kingdom - building habits prepare us to stand before God. You are going to cross a finish line someday. As you cross it, will God find you faithful? The faithful life is the successful life. It is the life God rewards with more.

The unfaithful servant is a warning to us all. He shows us how seriously God is about not taking Him serious. But I do not want to get lost in the unfaithful servant. We don't have to live like that. It is a warning of how not to live but there are two examples of how we should live. If I get lost in the first two servants and if I think about living faithful for my King, here is my take - away- **Abundance awaits the faithful!**

I cannot wait to meet my King. I have failed. I still fail. I am still growing. However, I am so hopeful that I will hear "Well done, good and faithful servant." Even if I do not hear that, I want to die trying. I wish I could go back and tell that punk 22year-old kid working at American Eagle to get his crap together. I wish I could tell him that the thrill of the "party" will not last and will take from you more than it will give to you. That was the darkest time of my life. That was the unfaithful servant portion of my life.

I cannot change that time in my life but I can use *this* portion of my life to invest into others. I can invest into the old me I see before me. I recently had lunch with an "old me." I was sitting across the table from a 22year-old trying to find himself. At similar ages we had similar demons and great opportunities before us. For him, it is the band life. He has a producer and management team. He and his band are pretty legit. But the band life is not guiding him to

Jesus. The conversation is more about his spiritual demons and less about the Holy Spirit. He is fighting. I have been there. He has talent, God -given talent. I caught myself looking at him and silently praying that God would get a hold of him. Why? Because a guy with demons who fully gives himself over to Jesus becomes a demon -stomping kingdom builder. I could see that potential in him. If he takes his passions and abilities from God and uses it to build God's kingdom, JOY will fill his life. He is at a crossroads; for God to take hold of his life, he will have to lose his hold on life.

Maybe you are at a crossroads. You are gifted. As a person of faith, God has gifted you. You have abilities. Will you let God take hold? Will you worship Him? Will you be found trustworthy? "I don't have talent. I have no ability." Send that lie back to the pit of hell. NOW. In Christ, you are His workmanship. In Christ, you have a spiritual gift. God does not make garbage. You are not garbage. I can say confidently in Christ that it is not a question of if you have ability or talents. The question is if you and I will waste our God-given talents on things that do not matter.

So maybe you need to close out this chapter by going to Google and typing in "spiritual gifts assessment." Please do it. There are 9,500,000 results for you to wade through. I am pretty sure you can find something on the first page! Once you have identified your spiritual gifts, DO SOMETHING ABOUT IT. Be the kingdom-building demon-stomper that God has created you to be. Share the gospel. Show love. Do not sit on your evangelistic hands. Jesus is coming back. This is how we are to be "successful" in the eyes of God!

RESULT #3: SUCCESS WITH MAN
BIBLICAL CASE STUDY

Let not steadfast love and faithfulness forsake you;
bind them around your neck; write them on the
tablet of your heart. So you will find favor and
good success in the sight of God and man."(Proverbs 3:3)

"It is not your business to succeed, but to do right: when
you have done so, the rest lies with God." **C.S. Lewis**

Biblical success is when God's heart and God's ways become my heart and my way. As we live this out, what can we expect? Having spent time examining the favor of God and success in the eyes of God, we now focus on success with man. What might God-given success in the sight of man look like?

Early in our marriage, Ava and I found out we were expecting our first child. We were married less than a year. She was 22, and I was 26. It was equally as stressful as it was exciting. On one of our first visits to the doctor, they found something concerning. Through a specialist, it was confirmed that my wife has a bicornuate uterus. Technically that is two uteri. For Ava, it is a severely misshapen uterus that appears to be two uteri. It leaves us with a 60% chance of losing a child. We are likely in the clear if the baby takes on the right side. If the baby takes on the left side, it is fatal. On that visit with the specialist, he looked at my wife and said, "Do you like wine? Cause if you are feeling stressed, drink a glass of red wine. Stress will increase your chances of losing this child." Cool, doc! Apparently, you do not know my enneagram 6 wife. You just caused more stress with that comment! Joy of a new life while fighting the feeling of drowning!

Have you been there? Are you there? You look around, and there is so much in life to take joy in. You see it, but you do not feel it. You know it is there, but the feeling of drowning is also present. We fight to get ahead yet live in the struggle where we cannot seem to get our heads above water. As we are drowning, we become nearsighted with God. Human nature is to focus on the problem and circumstances we find ourselves in and not on the One who has wrapped us in His arms. It is hard to keep a long view when pain is near. It is hard to stay humble and selfless through pain. Why? Whether it's you or me, I just want this pain to end. Yet, I hope we will see in this chapter that the humble don't mumble or grumble through pain. This type of humility leads to success by God with man. Joseph is living proof of this truth.

Genesis 41, our text for this chapter, begins with "After two whole years," which demands a little context. Joseph grew up with jealous brothers because he was legit, the favorite. His dad did not hide this fact; there was no "I love everyone equally." Joseph was the favorite. His brothers got jealous and went to kill him until one of them spoke up. So instead, they sold him into slavery. Can you imagine, sitting there "captured" by your brothers as they argue if they should kill you or sell you? What are you feeling? What is filling your head and what do you think about God? Are you staring at your brothers as you walk farther and farther from your homeland toward the horizon of the unknown? Finally, you arrive in Egypt and are sold into slavery to a military man. He is an officer in Egypt, a true man's man.

Newly on the job and a foreigner, you are crushing it. God is showing you favor with Potiphar. In every task he gives you, you find success. Then his wife takes a liking to you. She's staring you down and is all like "me likey;" Come to bed with me. You say no and refuse. She corners you. You run, but ugh, you leave a garment behind. She is embarrassed and uses the garment to spin a story that you tried to take advantage of her. "He said she said," when it's slave versus owner's wife, is a loss for Joseph. Come on, God. I did the right thing. I honored you. And now from top dog in the family to slave? Top dog in my master's house and now I find myself sitting in jail. You sit in prison innocent- no future trial. You just wait. You just sit.

Then one day as you are sitting there, two fellow inmates begin talking about dreams they had. God has gifted you with the ability to interpret dreams. You do. One is destined to die, and one will soon be released. It plays out exactly as you said. You asked the one who would soon be released for help. There is agreement. So ya, it has been two years that you have been waiting for this cupbearer, the guy who got released, to do good on his promise and help get you out.

Two years is a long time to sit in jail. It is an even longer time when you consider the challenging road that led to the jail cell. There has been nothing but hardship preceding this sentence. Did God forget me? Am I worth remembering? As you sit in these thoughts, Pharaoh has a disturbing dream. He is confused. The wise men of the day cannot figure it out. It is here the cupbearer remembers his promise and makes good on it.

> **9 Then the chief cupbearer said to Pharaoh, "I remember my offenses today. 10 When Pharaoh was angry with his servants and put me and the chief baker in custody in the house of the captain of the guard, 11 we dreamed on the same night, he and I, each having a dream with its own interpretation. 12 A young Hebrew was there with us, a servant of the captain of the guard. When we told him, he interpreted our dreams to us, giving an interpretation to each man according to his dream. 13 And as he interpreted to us, so it came about. I was restored to my office, and the baker was hanged." Genesis 41:9-13**

Pharaoh had called for the most intelligent humans to tell him what these dreams meant. Useless. Pharaoh needed to look to a jail cell where there is an inmate with proven success in this very area! No one would think to look to the prison for guidance, but there wisdom sits.

At my former church, my senior pastor got an email one day asking for a meeting with all the pastors. It was from someone in our church that was a negative Nelly and said off-the-wall things. Every church has em'! My pastor granted her the meeting. So, one afternoon all the pastors are in his office with her as she precedes to tell a "word from God" she had for us. I do not remember exactly what she said, but I do remember it being off the wall. What I saw as "off the wall" my older, wiser senior leader saw as heresy. What she had to say went directly against scripture. So her word from God was anything but a word from God since God will never contradict scripture. He spoke up firmly, and she left. After she left, he looked at us and said, "in light of this what might God be telling us?" Now in the room is the seniors' pastor, the discipleship pastor, and my senior pastor. I am the youth pastor. I am younger. In the pastoral sense, we all knew I would say wild stuff! So, I spoke up and said, "This lady is tripping. Why would we even give her the time of day?!" To which my pastor responded with words I will never forget: "Jason, if God can use a donkey to speak to people, I don't have to like the messenger to hear a needed message." That pearl of wisdom has always stuck with me.

We go through hard and troubling times. We have seasons of great confusion. Sometimes the people we think should help us do not. Sometimes unexpected wisdom comes from unexpected places. The wisdom God has for you and I may come from a negative nelly, a donkey or a jail cell. Are you willing to hear God from whatever voice it may be?

When you are confused, like Pharoah, sometimes God will send unlikely voices to guide us forward. For you and I, how do we know if God is speaking through someone? First, God gave us the Holy Spirit as a discerning spirit within us. Secondly, the word of God is a test to see if someone is speaking truth. Thirdly, we have an advocate before the Father, Jesus, to whom we can pray for wisdom. And lastly, there is the counsel of many. What are my spiritually led friends saying to me? Not those who would puff me up, but those willing to say the hard thing. If you are unwilling to say the hard thing to me, you are not a voice I can trust. Find those people who will speak love in the form of encouragement and love in the form of correction. Perhaps, not knowing your individual situation, wisdom has been expressed to you, but it was not from a desirable source or something you wanted to hear. What will you do about it?

14 Then Pharaoh sent and called Joseph, and they quickly brought him out of the pit. And when he had shaved himself and changed his clothes, he came in before Pharaoh. 15 And Pharaoh said to Joseph, "I have had a dream, and there is no one who can interpret it. I have heard it said of you that when you hear a dream you can interpret it." 16 Joseph answered Pharaoh, "It is not in me; God will give Pharaoh a favorable answer." 17 Then Pharaoh said to Joseph, "Behold, in my dream I was standing on the banks of the Nile. 18 Seven cows, plump and attractive, came up out of the Nile and fed in the reed grass. 19 Seven other cows came up after them, poor and very ugly and thin, such as I had never seen in all the land of Egypt. 20 And the thin, ugly cows ate up the first seven plump cows, 21 but when they had eaten them no one would have known that they had eaten them, for they were still as ugly as at the beginning. Then I awoke. 22 I also saw in my dream seven ears growing on one stalk, full and good. 23 Seven ears, withered, thin, and blighted by the east wind, sprouted after them, 24 and the thin ears swallowed up the seven good ears. And I told it to the magicians, but there was no one who could explain it to me." 25 Then Joseph said to Pharaoh, "The dreams of Pharaoh are one; God has revealed to Pharaoh what he is about to do. 26 The seven good cows are seven years, and the seven good ears are seven years; the dreams are one. 27 The seven lean and ugly cows that came up after them are seven years, and the seven empty ears blighted by the east wind are also seven years of famine. 28 It is as I told Pharaoh; God has shown to Pharaoh what he is about to do. 29 There will come seven years of great plenty throughout all the land of Egypt, 30 but after them there will arise seven years of famine, and all the plenty will be forgotten in the land of Egypt. The famine will consume the land, 31 and the plenty will be unknown in the land by reason of the famine that will follow, for it will be very severe. 32 And the doubling of Pharaoh's dream means that the thing is fixed by God, and God will shortly bring it about. 33 Now

therefore let Pharaoh select a discerning and wise man, and set him over the land of Egypt. 34 Let Pharaoh proceed to appoint overseers over the land and take one-fifth of the produce of the land of Egypt during the seven plentiful years. 35 And let them gather all the food of these good years that are coming and store up grain under the authority of Pharaoh for food in the cities, and let them keep it. 36 That food shall be a reserve for the land against the seven years of famine that are to occur in the land of Egypt, so that the land may not perish through the famine." Genesis 41:14-36

Had the cupbearer remembered Joseph immediately, he probably was not standing before Pharaoh. God's timing is perfect, yet up until this point, Joseph would not have felt this way. In the waiting, it is challenging to see the perfection of God's timing. Yet it is.

One morning you are sitting in jail, and all of a sudden, you are rushed before the king of the land. Classic. We have all been there, right? No! Hard to imagine. On the way to the king, Joseph has a makeover and stands before the king, not looking like someone who has been in jail. Although his appearance does not represent what he has been through, he has the humility of a lowly inmate. Only God can do this. Only God could get you from jail cell to throne room. Joseph knows this. When it comes to the dream? Yup, 'samsies.' Only God can interpret the dream. This is one of those problems in life where you can try to manufacture an answer, but only God can truly solve it. I love how Joseph frames these statements. He is speaking of God in a way that promises God will act. Joseph has a faith that breeds confidence. If I had spent the morning in jail, been lied about to get there and sold into slavery by my family, I am not sure I would speak of God with such confidence. Yet the faith of Joseph transcends circumstances.

This deep faith never offends Pharaoh. Joseph is taking a huge "risk" speaking so boldly. Pharaoh is seen as a deity for the nation. Yet, Joseph stands before him saying this is a message from the one TRUE God. This, given the theology of the land, is an insult to Pharaoh. However, as you and I know, Joseph speaks truth.

So, Joseph shares the truth of the situation and Pharaoh is better for it. Yup, these dreams are the one true God giving you a heads up. This is not judgment coming your way. This is a future reality that God is showing you grace by informing you, so you can prepare. This is a dream of prosperity and devastating tragedy, so be prepared. Do not squander this. Joseph goes a step beyond the interpretation to inform Pharaoh of the type of man he should look for to carry out the job ahead. It is a good plan for survival and economically advantageous to the king. From beginning to end, from jail cell to throne room, from the first hello to the last goodbye, through the highs and lows of life, Joseph is living a story for God's glory.

I mentioned this in an earlier chapter, but I want to mention this again. God's glory on display was never as magnified as when my brother lost his 14-month-old child. In his prepared comments at her funeral, I saw my brother stand in God's strength and thank Him for COVID. Not for COVID period, because we all know it was awful. But, he thanked God that because of COVID he was forced to work from home for 12 months of Charlotte's 14-month life. He did the math and thanked God for something like 2,470 extra hours given to him with his precious daughter. I saw him and my amazing sister-in-law raise their hands with tears flowing down her face while the worship team played "It is well." The room saw a story of God's glory being lived out before them in the midst of tragedy.

If we lived Joseph's life, what would be said of our attitude? What would be said of our perspective? Would we be resilient? Do we blame God or bring Him fame? Would this be the time we fight to "get ours" because this God thing has not worked out for us? When life has gone all wrong for so long, it is a challenge to declare a God that is in complete control. But this is precisely what Joseph did. He had all the reasons to question God but never seemingly does. Bitterness would have been natural and understandable, but Joseph does not take the bait. Joseph is humble through it all; it is in this humility that God receives all the glory. What is before you? You may not feel God's glory, but will you fight to bring Him glory despite your feelings? In your humility, will you let your story bring Him glory?

37 This proposal pleased Pharaoh and all his servants. 38 And Pharaoh said to his servants, "Can we find a man like this, in whom

is the Spirit of God?" 39 Then Pharaoh said to Joseph, "Since God has shown you all this, there is none so discerning and wise as you are. 40 You shall be over my house, and all my people shall order themselves as you command. Only as regards the throne will I be greater than you." 41 And Pharaoh said to Joseph, "See, I have set you over all the land of Egypt." 42 Then Pharaoh took his signet ring from his hand and put it on Joseph's hand, and clothed him in garments of fine linen and put a gold chain about his neck. 43 And he made him ride in his second chariot. And they called out before him, "Bow the knee!" Thus he set him over all the land of Egypt. 44 Moreover, Pharaoh said to Joseph, "I am Pharaoh, and without your consent no one shall lift up hand or foot in all the land of Egypt." 45 And Pharaoh called Joseph's name Zaphenath-paneah. And he gave him in marriage Asenath, the daughter of Potiphera priest of On. So Joseph went out over the land of Egypt.
Genesis 41:37-45

Remember again that Pharoah is seen by others and sees himself as a god. So Pharaoh calling Joseph one with the Spirit of God in him is no small thing. Through what he sees in Joseph, he sees him as able to carry out such a plan. He has the backing of God and he is not presumptuous. He is not power hungry. To give him power like this, he does not seem to be a threat to the throne. Pharaoh sees his humility. This all makes him "appointable." It is what grants him success with man. You are the man for the job, Joseph. Because God was with Joseph and Joseph was in turn faithful, God gave him success in the land of Egypt; Success to the point of being second in all the land. Second only to the king!

He submitted himself to God and was elevated by God. Oh, and he got a second wardrobe change that day! Oh, and he got the ancient version of a limousine in the chariot given to him, riding in style, my friend! He had men going before him, much like the secret service of our day. He is now a dignitary with the ability to sign legal documents. He is given a wife from a prominent family, giving him even more power and influence. Joseph had been faithful over all the little things God sent his way; now he would become a ruler over all the land of Egypt under Pharaoh. He surely was elevated by God!

He is still only around thirty years old, a young guy by today's standards. Are you reading this book because your twenties seemed aimless and painful? Feel like the situations you have been through cannot possibly be used by God? Stay humble. Stay hungry. God has a way of taking what was done over the decades and crafting God-sized moments out of them. Maybe (I do not know because I am not God), just perhaps, your twenties were a set up to your thirties.

Maybe you are in a place where you have seen God grant you success in this world. Do you praise God for the 'set up?' Think Joseph ever wished he could be overseeing Potiphar's house again? I have to imagine there were times Joseph longed to be restored to that oversight. Thank God He said no! "No Joseph, I need you to oversee this land; not a single house." I bet given how he would later speak to his brothers, Joseph clearly saw the hand of God with great satisfaction in that previous injustice. Have you gotten to that place?

My friends Josh and Krista Raj went through a particularly difficult season of life. Newly married, they moved from Pennsylvania to New Jersey to help us start the church. They lived in Krista's parent's basement. Saved money. Had a kid. Bought the dream starter home. One Christmas, not long after being in their home, they opened the door and found that a pipe had burst while they were gone. The way the pipe was configured in the house, it destroyed the house. It had to be largely gutted and redone. Now with a young child, they moved back into their parent's basement. There, they start fighting with the insurance company. Krista becomes pregnant again. They are in a basement with a young child, pregnant wife, and all while trying to serve God in this church plant. It was a mental and spiritual struggle for both of them. "God, we did all that was asked of us, and now we are punished for it?" They struggled to be patient in the storm. What now is looked back upon as a rough patch did not feel that way in the moment. It never does in the moment.

What they see now may not have been caught while they were in the storm. So, give yourself a little grace. It is hard to see God in the storm. Faith believes without seeing. Maybe that is what they mean when they say, "have little faith." In the storm, could they see the blessing of extra family time? They do now. In the storm, could they see the benefit of saving money while in the basement? They do now. In the storm, could they see the blessing of having a remolded and updated home that was able to be sold for a profit? They do now. Could they see what a gift it was to be surrounded by friends and family as they went through hardship? They do now! From the basement, it would have been hard to imagine that one day they would be in a new home, hosting a life group, where Jehovah's Witnesses would hear the gospel, people would come to faith, and many others would grow in their faith. God took them on a journey to get them where they needed to go. It was not easy, but it grew them.

God does not promise to shield us from all evil. This world is broken, and we are still in it. However, God is able to accomplish good through any circumstance. Serving an eternal God demands that we take an eternal view, allowing Him to work a process. You and I are both on a journey. We serve a God who will work through the generations. The family drama is part of the success journey when it is a set-up to get you to Egypt. Stay humble. The false accusation is part of the success journey when it is a set-up to get you to jail. Stay humble. The jail cell is part of the success journey when the jail cell is a set-up to bring you before the king. Stay humble. The time before the king, when God gets glory through your humility, perhaps becomes the ultimate set -up made possible only through the journey He has taken you on. Stay humble.

Here is what I hope we see in Joseph's story: **express humility to obtain success.**

Humility is an expression of dependency. Your success is inextricably linked to God. He is the lead. You are not. Humbly accept this and you will find success. In your years of plenty, stay humble. In your years of famine, stay humble. In the highs, stay humble. In the lows, stay humble. It is the humble that will know the grace of God.

As I was studying this section of God's word, I shot the elders of my church this question in a text, "how does humility keep us from grumbling in the midst of hardship?" It is a group of individuals that have lost homes, have wives struggling through health issues, some are fighting cancer, and some have experienced severe health struggles with their kids. As a group, they have experienced the highs and lows of life. Recently some have lost loved ones close to them, and some have recently been in financial woes. It is a group not foreign to pain. You do not have to dig deep to see how God has forged them spiritually through hardship.

Through the current and past hardships, they answered, "how does humility keep us from grumbling in the midst of hardship?" with some of the following responses:

> *I don't have control, we don't know what the outcome will be,*
> *humility forces us to trust the One who does control.*
> *God uses struggle as a springboard.*

> *Pain is selfish, keeps us in a heightened state of focusing on ourselves.*
> *Humility will push us beyond ourselves and will focus on*
> *something outside of ourselves.*

> *Complaining takes us back to the garden where we want to control.*

> *I want to fix everything and that is not possible. I have to*
> *humbly trust God through what I can't fix.*

> *Complaining implies I deserve better, entitlement is an aspect of*
> *grumbling and complaining. Humility says, "nothing is owed*
> *to me, I will be grateful for all that I have."*

I read over these texts over and over again. To me, they are like modern-day pearls of wisdom- wisdom that flows from life experiences and personal hardship. Much can be gained through the application of such wisdom.

Soon after we heard about Ava's bicornuate uterus, we found ourselves in the church's front office. I can't remember if it was right after the diagnosis or right after our first miscarriage as a result of it. Either way, we were young and impacted by the condition. In the front office was myself, my wife Ava, Fran Ward, and another co-worker. In the conversation my wife blurted out through the emotions, "I've been reading my Bible and praying. Why would this happen to me?" It was then a mature Fran Ward said, "you don't read your Bible and pray to keep you from hard times, you read your Bible and pray to get you through hard times." That has always stuck with me and is a reminder I need constantly.

What does your personal time with Jesus look like? Are you anchored to the King in the calm of the storm so you can remain anchored as the storm rages? Success with man is granted by our King. Success with Him and success with fellow man is often forged in hardship. How anchored in Him are you? Are your eyes on the storm or Jesus? Daily fix your eyes on Jesus. Live to bring Him glory in every situation He puts before you, and you are on the pathway to success. When two options are before you, pick the one that will bring God the most glory.

Anchor in, we all have a road ahead of us. May God receive all the glory.

GOD'S HEART AND GOD'S WAYS
IN FAVOR AND SUCCESS

Let not steadfast love and faithfulness forsake you;
bind them around your neck; write them on the
tablet of your heart. So you will find favor and
good success in the sight of God and man." (Proverbs 3-6)

"Those who have failed miserably are often the first to
see God's formula for success" **Erwin Lutzer**

iblical success is when God's heart and God's ways become my heart and my way.
As we live this out, what can we expect? Is what we expect of God
realistic? Do we have unrealistic expectations of God that have
become unmet expectations of God? Were we focused on achieving
something God never intended for us to achieve, leaving us to question
God's activity in our lives? Or perhaps these questions are not helpful
because you really haven't thought this way before. Following Jesus (part one
of this book) will cost you the typical human experience. Yet, we see God's
favor over our lives as an all-in when it is an either/or.

Let me illustrate it like this: I know beyond a shadow of a doubt that God
has led my wife and I to ministry and church planting. I knew God was
leading me to ministry in high school on a camping trip with my youth group.
I knew God led me to start a church at a Converge Church Planting
Assessment during a worship set with my wife. I had no idea what this calling
would cost me in life. I do not have normal Easters. My kids do not wake up,

find Easter baskets, get on cute clothes, eat brunch, then hit a church service. I am a pastor, and my wife serves alongside me. My kids wake up at 6:45 AM, get on whatever is presentable, and then head to the church where we serve as a family. We have an evening church service, so we do not make Easter dinner on Sunday- we do it the Saturday before. We do not get weekend trips to the lake as a family because I work most every Sunday. There are no weekend getaways for us. What I see as everyday things in other people's lives are anything but ordinary for us. But it is where God has called us. If I strive for a typical Easter and weekends away, I would not be able to accomplish what God has asked me to accomplish. And with all this, I am blessed.

As we close out this journey, having examined the kind of life God would see as successful, what is God's involvement in my life as I move forward? If I am experiencing God's favor and success, what should I expect that experience to look like?

Experiencing God's favor and success will...

... redefine how you think about favor and success. Naturally, this flows into the first thing experiencing God's favor and success will do to you; it will redefine how you think about it. It is the premise of this book and how God has moved in my own life. This sentiment is the specific premise of this section, so why heighten it as one of the defining marks? There are moments I am talking to my wife or my kids where I will say, "I am your husband" or "I am your Dad." At this stage in our lives, that truth has been clearly established and is unquestionable. However, stating the apparent truth focuses and sets the tone for the rest of the conversation. This is why we are starting with "experiencing God's favor and success will redefine how you think about favor and success." This forces us to reconsider our preconceived notions.

Noah had God's favor and had to build a boat.
Mary had God's favor and lived with a reputation as sexually immoral.
Abraham was successful and had to pack up everything to go to a new land.
Job was successful and became a target for the evil one.

These are just a few quick instances that come to my mind. Maybe I need to rethink my own life. Maybe my hard life is a favored life. Perhaps as I allow my understanding of favor and success to be redefined, feelings will follow.

I may not feel God's favor or success right now, but is that because I do not view favor and success biblically? Perhaps, in this chapter, right thinking will lead to the right feeling.

In Acts 8, we see the church expanding to new regions of the world. People are coming to know Jesus, they are being baptized, and they are receiving the Holy Spirit. One onlooker, Simon the sorcerer, was amazed by the power of the Holy Spirit. As a sorcerer, of course, the power of the Holy Spirit would be impressive. So what does he do? He asks Philip how he can buy it. For real. Specifically, he wanted to buy the ability to lay hands on people and give them the Holy Spirit. As you can expect, this was met with harsh rebuke. But, as a sorcerer, the Holy Spirit could get him rich. In his mind, this would have been a good business investment. It would have made him successful. Simon saw Philip as successful. Philip saw Jesus as Lord. Everything fell into place behind the Lordship of Jesus Christ. What Simon saw as a matter of money, business, power and success was not a matter of any of these things. It was simply what happens to people who submit to the Lordship of Jesus Christ- they receive the Holy Spirit. Simon's thinking needed to be corrected.

I am writing this on a Monday morning. Yesterday at church we had about 175 people. My "number two" preached for me and preached a way better sermon than I would have on 2 Samuel 13. So much of my pastoral upbringing would look at yesterday as a failure. We are under 200 people. The Lead Pastor is not the best preacher at the church. Wellspring Bayville was chaotic last night with families and tutoring (for real) happening during the sermon. I had a mom and dad talking with a friend outside who missed the whole sermon. I could go on and on, and that is the point. It would be easy for me to sit here early on a Monday morning and feel like yesterday was a failure. That's my problem, I take "needs improvement" to places of "failure."

Yesterday, we had a handful of new people. Yesterday we had an influx of young people at church. We had a 19-year-old invite friends. We had a lady who has come every single week for about 3 months receive a study Bible from two female mentors. She is moving and we only got to be part of her journey for a short time, but these two ladies made the most of this short time with her and her spiritual journey. We set up a meal train for someone in a life group who just had a kidney transplant. That person getting tutored is a young man getting his GED so he can get his life back on track. I am part of a system where I am not the main guy, but other strong leaders can flourish. Although not a win for my ego it is a win for the kingdom. We had countless people jump at the opportunity to buy items for families in need that we are going to give out at the end of the month. We had a family asking to be part of a life group. We had about 60 people take "Go Deeper Guides" to use throughout the week to go deeper in the study of God's word. Again, I could go on and on.

If you have a personality like mine, too often I walk around feeling like a failure when I should pause and see the work of God at hand. Those times I feel like a failure in the day-to-day, I need to step back, gain perspective, and work on improvement, while guarding against feelings of failure. God is moving but if I do not understand how He moves, I will never see it or feel it.

... *put you on a mission.* Why does God grant favor and success? It is to put you on mission. It is to guide you forward. It trains you and prepares you. I cannot think of a single instance in scripture where God granted favor and success "just because" or for someone's sheer enjoyment. I cannot think of a single example where God is acting like the host of some game show saying "Johnny, tell them what they have won." 1 Kings 17 with the widow of Zarephath, she had a great need. God met that need with oil and flour that did not run out. It is written into the pages of Scripture to highlight the favor of God and His great faithfulness. It was not a get-rich scheme for this widow. It was provision.

Remember in Chapter 3, when we mentioned the Derek Carr contract? Yes, he talked about tithing, a habit that I wish more people had. But what really caught my attention in that news conference was when he said, "The exciting thing for me, moneywise, honestly, if this money is going to help a lot of people... I'm very thankful to have it- that it's in our hands because it's going to help people; not only in this country, but in a lot of countries around the world. That's what's exciting to me." He saw this as a gift from God (given his tithing comments) and saw it as a good thing in his hands because of how he would be able to bless people around the world. This is a guy who saw the blessing of God from a missional perspective. This is one way to be put on mission through blessing.

Yet there are other ways as well. Stephen was favored and selected by the Apostles to help widows. He was a great man. This favor set the stage for him to die for his faith. The Apostles had God's favor in their ability to heal. They were arrested. They were beaten. When released, they said, "Then they left the presence of the council, rejoicing that they were counted worthy to suffer dishonor for the name." Acts 5:41

The point: great things can happen in ministry. Greatness in ministry often is God's favor meeting our faithfulness. The result? Suffering. But Jason, isn't this about being put on mission? Yes. The call of Christ and the call of ministry is a call to suffer. Paul David Tripp says in his book *Lead*, "Ministry leadership is not a fortress against spiritual attack; it's the front line." Here he describes that Christian leadership- following Christ- is a call to suffer. As leaders, we expect favor and success to guide us to places where suffering is avoided. No. God's favor will often lead us to a place of suffering. It is the literal way of Christ.

The Apostle Paul said it best in Philippians 1:12-14:

> **12 I want you to know, brothers, that what has happened to me has really served to advance the gospel, 13 so that it has become known throughout the whole imperial guard and to all the rest that my imprisonment is for Christ. 14 And most of the brothers, having become confident in the Lord by my imprisonment, are much more bold to speak the word without fear.**

Paul experienced countless persecutions. He was not occasionally persecuted; for him it was a way of life. How did he see it? As God's favor to proclaim the gospel message of Jesus Christ. Put me in prison? Fine, the prison guards will know the name of Jesus! Through hardship I will proclaim boldly and the result? Others will be motivated to greater boldness in sharing the gospel.

Maybe God's favor, like previously stated, will bring hardship to your life. Will you proclaim the name of Jesus? Will you see a challenging assignment from God as His favor? If you are in great need and God meets you in that place, will you tell a story of God's glory?

… look different for each follower. We see how God favors other people and we want that favor. Yet, God will bless people differently. It is His right as Lord of the universe to do so. We are called to run the race marked out for us (Hebrews 12). I am not called to run your race; I am called to run my race. The way God blesses you to run the race He has laid out for you is different from how He will bless the race He has marked out for me. There are aspects of the Christian faith that are universally true and expected, yet play out differently for each believer. We are all called to disciple others. The manner may be different for each situation. We are all called to be in God's word. How I dig into the word of God (journaling, prayer walks, writing, preaching) may look different than it does for you. We are all called to evangelize and share the gospel. How? Some as street evangelists. Some through deep relationships. At this point in my life, I do not feel called to share the gospel in Africa so I do not expect God to bless me so that I could be able to do that. However, He is blessing some to do that. My blessing looks different because my call is different.

Paul looked at the single, childless life as a blessing for the ministry he was able to do. Others were blessed with kids older in life as a display of God's promise and great power. Different calls, different forms of favor, and different blessings. Remember the parable of talents? Each servant was given talents according to his abilities. One got 10, one got 5 and the other 1. They were given different talents but had the same expectation. Build upon them!

I have two boys, Landon and Brady. They are blessed in different ways. Landon is a very intelligent kid. School comes easy to him. Last marking period he got all B's. I was very angry because he did not live up to his ability. It showed he did not try or apply himself. Brady on the other hand got three A's and I was overjoyed. He struggles in school. Sit down to do homework with him and you will want to go play in traffic. Don't tell him this, but I would be overjoyed if he just got straight B's. He is more gifted in sports. Both kids go to school. Both kids play sports. I give money for grades and I give money for all-star teams. In a given year, they both have the opportunity to make the same amount of money, if they live up to their potential within their given blessings. They are blessed differently but the expectation is the same: live up to the way God has blessed you (live up to your God-given potential).

Can I restate something given this point? STOP COMPARING YOURSELF TO OTHERS. Here is where there's room for comparison: "Be imitators of me, as I am of Christ." (1 Corinthians 11:1). Comparisons that draw you closer to Jesus and help you become more like Jesus, GREAT! I look across the room as I type and see my wife reading her Bible. If this was a foreign practice to me and seeing this motivated me to get into the word of God, then GREAT! But when we start comparing blessings, allowing doubt, anger, and jealousy to creep in, danger is lurking. God will bless people differently. Others will have different talents. Others will have different prosperity. Others will have different struggles. You will have a season of suffering while others have a season of plenty and vice versa. God is at work in all cases.

Catch a scene from the end of John 21 and do not just read the words of Jesus. I want you to say it out loud and *hear* the words of Jesus:

> **20 Peter turned and saw the disciple whom Jesus loved following them, the one who also had leaned back against him during the supper and had said, "Lord, who is it that is going to betray you?" 21 When Peter saw him, he said to Jesus, "Lord, what about this man?" 22 Jesus said to him, "If it is my will that he remain until I come, what is that to you? You follow me!" 23 So the saying spread abroad among the brothers that this disciple was not to die; yet Jesus did not say to him that he was not to die, but, "If it is my will that he remain until I come, what is that to you?"** John 21:20-23

Peter and Jesus just had a very powerful conversation, if you know the scene. Peter instantly takes his eyes off Jesus and sees John. What crept in? Comparison. What about him?! Hear the words that Jesus said to him, words I feel through the Spirit; Jesus is saying to us often: *What is that to you? You follow Me!* What is that to you? You follow me! Say it. Think about the last time you fell into the comparison trap. Got the situation in your mind? Now, say these words out loud, *"What is that to you? You follow Me!"* This must become a habit in our lives.

… cost you. Favor and blessing will cost you. The prosperity preachers never focus on this point. Favor and blessing cost Mary her reputation. Favor and blessing cost Noah 120 years of his life. Favor and blessing cost Job in the form of attacks from the evil one. Favor and blessing led Paul to beatings. Favor and blessing led Abraham to pack up and move. Favor and blessing led David to donate millions to build the temple. The early church saw suffering and martyrdom as a blessing (queue the verse *counted worthy to suffer…*).

Part of the cost is in the expectation. Jesus says in Luke 12, "Everyone to whom much was given, of him much will be required, and from him to whom they entrusted much, they will demand the more." This means you and I will stand before God and be held accountable differently. There are expectations on my life that are not on your life. There are ways in which I have been blessed that I will be held accountable for which will not be true of you. The question remains for both of us, "Did we squander the blessings God gave to us?" Like we said, God's blessing and favor puts us on mission. There is a cost to this. You must DO SOMETHING with the gifts God has bestowed upon you. Landon is blessed with smarts- do something about it and get good grades. Brady is blessed with athletic abilities- do something about it and make an all-star team.

I was blessed as a church planter in unheard-of ways. There are so many stories behind this, but let me give you the highlights. My sending church gave us $275,000. We had a VERY talented core team of around 20 people. We had a launch team of about 90 people. The core team raised $90,000. A church from New Hampshire gave us $50,000. I had a denomination providing training, coaching, and money, if needed. Less than a month after launching I had another full-time staffer and 4 part-timers. Yo, hashtag blessed, y'all! Church planters hear this and salivate. They hear this and think, "I want this and I need this." NOPE! You need what God gives you. And you need to make much of what God gives you. Unhealthy me took the immense pressure I felt from such a blessing and nearly put myself in the grave. I feared the thought of failing in -light of such a great blessing greatly. I lost joy, fun, and excitement; becoming militant, driven, and demanding. In light of these blessings, a big launch was rightfully expected. In light of these blessings, were there baptisms? Salvation? This is all work of the Holy Spirit, but there was an expectation that the blessing would be used towards this end. After all, the Holy Spirit is the greatest kingdom building gift we have! The expectation of the blessing was not for a big bank account. The expectation of the blessing was not to entertain the people coming through our doors, keep them happy and keep them coming. The expectation was to build a church reaching into a community void of gospel impact.

The cost that I am describing is that you must use the blessing (cost) to push the kingdom forward (mission). The favor and blessing God shows you in light of your godly, blameless character may come across as suffering as He calls you to the mission field. It may feel like suffering as He calls you to the neighbor who for a season will make fun of you, before turning his life to Christ. It may feel like suffering as you get the promotion with demands on your schedule so you can help fund a local youth outreach program. On the other hand, the favor and blessing God shows you in light of your blameless character may not result in a new car, house or bank account, but a demanding job assignment for gospel advancement. Will you take up your cross daily, with joy, because you have been counted worthy to suffer?

If God has blessed you with incredible resources, will you allow yourself to take on the additional costs of kingdom building? Did God bless you just to pad a bank account or use your skill set to make a name for yourself? Or perhaps He has shown you favor in skill and finances trusting you to build His kingdom. Was this not the rich young ruler found in the gospels (Mark 10, Luke 18, and Matthew 19)? He was blessed with money and skills. He was young and had it all going on. Jesus said great, sell it all, come follow me and you will have treasure in heaven. Use your 'treasure' and I will give you heavenly treasure. He walked away, unrighteous, because of what he was unwilling to do. God has blessed you with skills and finances. Are you willing or unwilling to build His kingdom, to follow Him, and receive treasure in heaven?

... grow you. God is deeply concerned with your growth. Rick Warren is credited to have said, "God is more interested in your character than your comfort. God is more interested in making your life holy than He is in making your life happy." When hardship comes your way, God will use it to build your character. The same is true with favor and blessings. Favor and blessing is not solely to make you happy: that is a byproduct of something ultimately about building your character. God is a character-building God. Paul says in Philippians 1:6: "And I am sure of this, that he who began a good work in you will bring it to completion at the day of Jesus Christ." Have you allowed the blessings of God to be part of the work of God? Again, I cannot think of a single example where God blessed simply to bless. He is not a genie. Any time He blesses, there is a need. It may be a widow who lacks resources (need) and God blesses her with flour and oil. Or there is a kingdom need where God blesses a kingdom-minded person to fill that need. Or there is character within a person that needs to be developed, so God blesses a person as a way to build that character. Or he blesses Jacob to prove to others that He is with him.

By nature, I suck financially. In my earlier 20's I had an unpaid credit card that I had maxed out. I remember vividly the phone calls from collection agencies, followed by phone calls to my mom sobbing for help. I was as unwise as you can get with finances. Fast forward to marriage and early on, my wife and I shared a lack of wisdom financially. Ava, when you read this, remember that time we had $9 in our bank account and had to feed my family that randomly came to visit?! Good times. Then, over the course of a few years God used two events to help shape us: a new job and Financial Peace University (FPU). We took Dave Ramsey's FPU and learned healthy money habits. The blessing of knowledge grew us. Then Ava got a new job through the blessing of a friend who walked with her into a new industry. Ava now makes roughly 40% more than I do. It is a financial blessing, along with the knowledge we have gained of finances that has allowed us to pay off all our debt, minus the house. Ok, great. We are blessed financially. Do you think our character has been built through it? At times, no. We are sinful humans. But at times, yes. Ava is self-employed so routine IRS audits are expected. We have only been audited once. Wanna know why? They did not believe our giving records. When someone who I had struggled with in the past needed a car, it was through character -building prayer that we decided to provide him with a car worth $7,250, because it was the right thing to do.

Does God bless you to grow your things or your character? God blesses and will show you favor financially. Will you allow it to develop or weaken your character? The enemy wants to take God's blessings and have you walk away from God in shame, like the rich young ruler. The enemy wants to take the blessings of God and destroy any spiritual growth you have experienced. The enemy wants to take the blessings of God and get you to worship the blessing (idol) instead of the One who blesses. God wants to grow you as He grows His kingdom. I have heard it said, "God blesses us to be a blessing to others. Advance His kingdom, and reveal His love through the gift of salvation in Christ." Your character grows as you take God's blessings with open hands to bless others. In speaking of character and spiritual blessings, Peter says, "As each has received a gift, use it to serve one another" (1 Peter 4:10A). In the hands of God, have His blessings grown your character? Or, in the hands of the enemy, has our character been destroyed? Are you serving yourself or serving others? It takes immense spiritual character to use God's blessings to selflessly bless others. Perhaps this is why God has blessed you- to build selfless character within you!

... test you. Often when we experience God's favor and given success, we will be tested. The testing can come in a variety of forms but it will all center around worship. If the blessing remained, will you worship the blessing or the God of the blessing? If the blessing went away, would you still worship God? If asked to sacrifice blessing in the worship of the Creator, would you?

Consider Solomon. Towards the end of his life we read this about him, *"For when Solomon was old his wives turned away his heart after other gods, and his heart was not wholly true to the LORD his God, as was the heart of David his father."* (1 Kings 11:4) Solomon was blessed with great wealth, insight, fame, and prestige. No other earthly king ever had the favor of God quite as Solomon did. He had it all. He started to marry foreign women- something forbidden for God's people (1 Kings 11:2). Solomon allowed for, encouraged and helped make a way for his foreign wives to worship their foreign pagan gods. The king of Israel literally using the financial blessings of God to build altars to foreign gods. The blessing led to a divided heart and the downfall of Solomon. When he died, he did not die a man wholly given over to God in worship.

Or consider Job who had wealth, a large family, and a strong relationship with God. Satan is roaming the earth, then has a conversation with God and says, *"Then Satan answered the Lord and said, "Does Job fear God for no reason? 10 Have you not put a hedge around him and his house and all that he has, on every side? You have blessed the work of his hands, and his possessions have increased in the land. 11 But stretch out your hand and touch all that he has, and he will curse you to your face."* (Job 1:9-11). Satan acknowledges God's blessings of Job and says this is why he worships Him. In Satan's thinking, Job only worships God because He blesses and not simply because of God Himself. So, the test. Take it all away and will Job still worship God? Yes. Through the journey, Job maintained his integrity; he worshiped His God and God double blessed him at the conclusion of the story.

Or consider Abraham who was blessed with Isaac at an old age. In Genesis 22 God asks Abraham to sacrifice Isaac to him. Abraham immediately heads out and when they got to the mountain, Abraham says to his servant: *"Then Abraham said to his young men, "Stay here with the donkey; I and the boy will go over there and worship and come again to you."* (Genesis 22:5) Abraham saw what was about to take place as worship. You know the story, Isaac and Abraham are walking up the mountain. Isaac sees there is no sacrifice and inquires to Abraham about where the sacrifice is. Abraham trusts God and says that God will provide it. They build the altar. He lays Isaac on it. The knife is coming down. And God says, *"Do not lay your hand on the boy or do anything to him, for now I know that you fear God, seeing you have not withheld your son, your only son, from me."* (Genesis 22:12). God saw a God-fearing man. Abraham was blessed. What would he decide? Would he love blessing more than obeying his God? No. He was willing to love God and obey God even if it meant sacrificing the blessing. That is worship.

As mentioned, I once had worship described to me as "worthship." The point the person was trying to make is when we worship we are ascribing God worth. We have talked in great depth about worship in this book. There is a reason for that. Every moment of our day, there is a cosmic battle vying for our worship. Every moment, we are to decide who gets our worship. Every moment we are ascribing worth to the Creator or countless other entities. When you get godly counsel and ungodly counsel, you ascribe God worth by taking the godly counsel. When there are competing voices in your head, you ascribe God worth when you allow His voice to be the loudest voice. When you have been blessed and have a moment to build your kingdom, your platform, and your fame, you ascribe God worth when you build His kingdom, allow Him to be your platform, and live for His fame. You have been blessed with knowledge. How will you ascribe God worth in that place? You have been blessed with influence. How will you ascribe God worth in that place? You have been blessed with family. How will you ascribe God worth in that place?

You are living in a spiritual war right now as you read this. Who will get your worship? You have not been to church in a while cause the blessing of kids got you so busy. Who is getting your worship? You used to have conversations with your unsaved friends about Jesus; now you can't remember the last time you talked to someone about Jesus. Who is getting your worship? You used to make time for reading God's word, but you were blessed with that promotion eating up your time. Who is getting your worship? Perhaps you are in the middle of a worship test and you didn't even realize it!

... benefit you. When we experience God's favor, blessing and success, we will benefit from the experience. I know, I know, "Jason, we are talking about God's favor, blessing, and success, but why would anyone want what you are describing?!" I get it. Much of what we have said thus far seems almost negative. Will Favor cost us? Test us? Require us to work on a mission? Yes. So let me ask you before we get into the benefits: Why does this seem so negative? Does it seem negative in the backdrop of prosperity, gospel, preachers? Of course, their message is more appealing. It is a lot of giving and little take. It is a message that fills stadiums and pads bank accounts. Do I believe God's blessing and favor will benefit you? I certainly do.

Did God's favor benefit Job? YES. He was literally a doubly blessed man in the end. Did God's favor benefit Joseph? He was second in command, his family was taken care of, he was well fed during a famine, and he had the king's ear. Did God bless Egypt under Joseph? Yes, it was the seven years of great blessing that proved to be a benefit during the seven years of famine. Wealthy women supported the Lord's ministry. Abraham was wealthy. Barnabas was a land owner who had land to sell.

Never apologize for the blessing of God. Never apologize when God chooses to bless, show favor, and grant success. If God is sovereign, and He is, never apologize for what God has ordained.

My wife does very well for herself as a real estate appraiser. I never apologize for that. She works hard. She puts the time in. She seeks to honor God in the blessing. In her line of work, work is not guaranteed. God can make it rain jobs or there can be a shortage of jobs. God is good either way. I do not apologize to anyone when we take a vacation. I do not apologize to anyone for the house we live in. I funnel all financial decisions through my faith. People will make comments; it is often people who do not give to the church. They do not see my bank account; they do not see how much we give to the local church each year. I do not apologize for the utilization of God's blessing because I can confidently stand before God with how we honor Him in our finances.

God's blessing and favor on your life will come in many different forms, but of this I am confident, you benefit from being blessed by God. As Christian's, we are blessed for trusting in God because the One in whom we trust is a great blessing to us (Jeremiah 17). We are blessed to know God because in knowing God we are kept by God (Numbers 6). Is not the future of the Christian one of great blessing? For the Christian, this life is the worst it will ever be for us, but for the non-Christian, this life is the best it will ever be. Think about that. Are we to apologize for that? Will not eternity be a great "benefit" to the believer? Romans 2:4 says the kindness of the Lord leads to repentance. God is kind. God is love. I know this in the person of Jesus Christ. Through Christ, I know God as Father. He is my warrior. He fights for me. I have access to the throne to talk with my Father. In Christ, I have an advocate before the Father. I AM A BLESSED MAN.

How are you blessed and favored? How could it benefit you? God's favor and blessing could help when you have a great need that God meets. God's favor and blessing could help you when others respect you, because God has given you great wisdom. God's favor and blessing could benefit you in opportunities God opens up for you. God's favor could benefit you in the form of finances, stuff, knowledge, fame, opportunity, and position. The benefit of God's blessings can take many different forms, but know this for sure- it all comes from God.

Growing up, my parents divorced when I was in the 4th grade. I am the oldest, and as the oldest, I had a unique front-row seat to the divorce. I did not see it as a blessing or a benefit. My mom was raised in a strict Christian home and carried some of that "strictness" into our home. Like I think I mentioned, I have missed all-star games when they happened on a Sunday morning during church hours. I did not see it then, but the dependency on God's word I learned through that divorce serves me now as a great blessing. I did not see it then, but the lessons I learned to value women as a "mama's boy" serves me now as I love my wife. I did not see it then, but learning the value of church through hardship, serves me now as a great blessing. Every Sunday in that old church, my Pastor Rick Huntley, would have us sing a hymn known as The Doxology. The opening line says "Praise God from whom all blessings flow." I would bet my life that I sang that song more than once in a grumbling tone. But now I see it, feel it, and praise my God for it.

Sometimes we cannot see the benefits that are before us and so we lose sight of the blessing. In the moment, I did not see the blessing of extra time with my kids through COVID, but it was a blessing I kind of miss. When my Grandfather was stuck at JFK airport 90 minutes from where I live, I did not see traveling up there to get him, and then having to figure out how to get him home as a blessing, but, turns out, that was the last time I saw him alive. It was a blessing I now see as a great 'benefit.' God's blessings are a benefit to us, big or small. We may not see it as a benefit in the moment, but in time, may God give us eyes to see. From God, and only God, do all blessings flow.

What is Biblical success? *Biblical success is when God's heart and God's ways become my heart and my way.* God is the God of blessing. God is a God of success. God is a God of favor. As we close out this chapter and as we have been talking for 12 chapters now, we need to realign our heart, mind, and ways to live, think and act as Christ, as if He were living our lives. Let me close this chapter with something Solomon wrote in Proverbs 30:8-9:

"Remove far from me falsehood and lying; give me neither poverty nor riches; feed me with the food that is needful for me, lest I be full and deny you and say, "Who is the Lord?" or lest I be poor and steal and profane the name of my God."

When I was young, striving after fame and riches seemed like everything to me. It seemed like the number one way in which God would bless. Now? It actually kind of scares me to think about winning the lottery because I am afraid it would change me for the worse. If I became famous, I do not know if I would make it all about God. I hope I would. The sad truth is that Solomon, who wrote this, never lived it out. The blessings and favor and prosperity gospel friends preached of served to be his ruin. As God's heart and God's ways become my way and my heart, my prayer is that God would give me neither poverty nor riches, lest I deny God and say "Who is the Lord.?" May I always find those quiet walks in the morning with my dog as a blessing. May I always find my house to be enough. May I always see quiet times of prayer with my wife in the morning as a blessing. May I always find my kids' sports as a blessing when I am forced to disconnect from work.

Jesus you are enough; everything else is just cake. Thank you.

CONCLUSION

Semisonic perhaps said it best, "Closing time, every new beginning comes from some other beginning's end." Is this the end to the journey, just the beginning, or both? As we close out this book, what do you need to focus on? Where is your heart misaligned with God? What are you doing that you now see is not the way of Christ? What will you do about it?

My Grandfather died on April 24th, 2022. He died as I was writing Chapter 12 of this book. He was older, but died unexpectedly. In March, he was in Peru hiking the mountains and seeing old friends. I was close to him. I am in ministry largely because of him. My grandfather was a missionary in Peru and a pastor in Pennsylvania. I close this book with him heavy on my mind. Last year he finished his only book, *The Making of a Model; on Becoming a Living Image of Jesus Christ.* Jesus was everything to him. I want Jesus to be everything to me. I hope He is everything to you.

On April 24th, as my Grandfather took his last breath, I was in Brazil. It was my first time in South America. I was preaching to a church about John 21 and encouraging the audience to love Jesus and follow Him. I encouraged them to stop the comparison game, compare themselves to Jesus and Jesus alone; becoming more like Him along the way. My Grandfather wanted nothing more than to honor God with his life and he longed to do so in South America. So, as my Grandfather's spirit left this earth, I was in South America preaching Jesus. As I look to carry on my Grandfather's legacy, can I share with you the two most important lessons I learned from him?

First, it is all about Jesus. As I type from my kitchen table, to my right is a brownish orange Bible. If my house was burning down, I would be tempted to run by my family to grab it. Ava, when you read this, I am mostly kidding ha! It is the Bible my Grandfather gave to me when I graduated from high school. I was heading to Bible school to begin preparing for ministry. The Bible he gave me was his preaching Bible; it was also his father's (my great grandfather's) preaching Bible. It is a keepsake for me that reminds me of the legacy I am a part of. When my grandfather gave me this Bible it came with a note that I have since lost. He said, "if they leave thinking my, what a wonderful sermon or my, what a wonderful preacher, you have failed. But if they leave thinking, my, what a wonderful Savior, you have succeeded." It is a comment he spoke to me often. These are words I take to heart. This life, success in life, is all about Jesus.

Secondly, it is all about people. My grandfather was quirky; there is no way around it. Many did not know how to take him. Do you know who learned to "take him?" Those that could see through the quirkiness and see a man who loved people. He wanted the big church, but it never came. He often felt like a failure. He wanted a significant ministry in Peru, but it never came. He often felt like a failure. I was blessed to officiate his funeral. Can I tell you what I saw? I saw about 25 of his neighbors come out to honor his life—25 neighbors from a small quiet street in Tilton, NH. My grandfather may not have impacted the masses, but he taught me how to influence the person next door. What good is a big name and big stage if the people next to me do not know of Jesus Christ? When I die, I hope all of Holly Park comes out. Why? That is my neighborhood, representing those I am closest to in proximity. I saw that in my grandfather's life, and I want it in my life. My grandfather taught me that the "love thy neighbor" thing is perhaps the best way to live as a model of Jesus Christ. My grandfather stands before God, not as a failure, but as a child of the King of Kings. If Christ is in you, we may fail, but we are never failures. Grandpa, I wish you could have seen all your neighbors there- you had a more significant impact than you could ever know.

One day, like my Grandfather, my life will cross a finish line. But, will it be a finish line that has honored Christ? Will I have lived a life that feels successful or that Christ determines is successful? So one last time, Biblical success is when God's heart and God's ways become my heart and my way. Proverbs 3:3-4 says: *Let not steadfast love and faithfulness forsake you; bind them around your neck; write them on the tablet of your heart. So you will find favor and good success in the sight of God and man.*

The book has now concluded, and the journey forward now begins.

APPENDIX 1: A POST FROM MY GRANDFATHER'S FACEBOOK ON JULY 18TH, 2019, SINCE READ GRAVESIDE AT HIS FUNERAL.

CERTAINTY IN THE AGE OF CONFUSION

With America in turmoil, there is much about the future that leaves me confused and uncertain. But I am pleased that in this age of skepticism I am able to face the future with confidence for there are some issues for which I have no doubt.

First of all, I am convinced that TRUTH IS KNOWABLE.

This is a great strength to me for the sentiment of this age is that truth is relative, and no one can know anything for sure. Not so! Jesus said, "You shall know the truth and the truth shall set you free." Truth, truth that determines who I am, why I am here, and where I am going, has been disclosed in Jesus Christ. He is the One Who makes sense of it all.

Secondly, and equally important to my well-being, is the fact that I have been granted THE POWER OF CHOICE.

I have been created with a free will. Not even God is going to coerce me into doing something I don't want to do. He invites my allegiance; He offers His strength; He promises an eternal future. But He leaves the choice to accept or reject everything He offers up to me. And accordingly, I have taken Him at His word, and I have not been disappointed. It is, indeed, a privilege to serve the Living God.

And then there is this. I am certain that I AM WHO I'M SUPPOSED TO BE, and that is good!

I have resolved to accept myself just as I AM. Warts and all, my imperfections notwithstanding, I have finally been able to believe in myself and enjoy my status in life without complaint. There is for me, until my death, no brighter tomorrow. My bright tomorrow is here and now. Until the day I stand in God's presence, I am comfortable with who and where I am in life.

Which brings me to a fourth certainty. I WILL SOON DIE.

This truth has made a major impact on my perspective. My days are numbered. But I face the prospect of death with excitement and anticipation. "In my Father's house are many mansions," Jesus said, "and I go to prepare a place for you that where I am you may be also."

If you are able to attend my funeral, you will encounter a celebration to rival any you have ever experienced. Cheers instead of tears, laughter in place of mourning, happiness rather than sorrow. Another of God's children has gone home; three cheers for a life fulfilled and complete!

And, finally, the anchor to all of this is the conviction that GOD IS.

On this also I have no doubt. My evidence is found in the resurrection of Jesus Christ. His resurrection, provable beyond doubt to anyone who will accept the record, validates His life and message. "No one has ever seen God," wrote the Apostle John, "but the one and only Son... has made him known." I believe in God because Jesus believed in God. That settles it for me.

In this age of confusion, the uncertainties of life haunt me no longer. I have met the Master and knowing Him has changed everything. After eighty years of living through some of life's most difficult experiences, I can tell you that serving Jesus Christ has made all the difference in my world. Indeed, God is good!

About Kharis Publishing

Kharis Publishing, an imprint of Kharis Media LLC, is a leading Christian and inspirational book publisher based in Aurora, Chicago metropolitan area, Illinois. Kharis' dual mission is to give voice to under-represented writers (including women and first-time authors) and equip orphans in developing countries with literacy tools. That is why, for each book sold, the publisher channels some of the proceeds into providing books and computers for orphanages in developing countries so that these kids may learn to read, dream, and grow. For a limited time, Kharis Publishing is accepting unsolicited queries for nonfiction (Christian, self-help, memoirs, business, health and wellness) from qualified leaders, professionals, pastors, and ministers. Learn more at: https://kharispublishing.com/